ONLY ENTERTAINM

The idea of entertainment is a guiding principle for both makers and audiences of films, television programmes and other media. Yet, while entertainment is often derided or praised, the concept itself is often taken for granted. *Only Entertainment* explores entertainment *as* entertainment, asking how and whether an emphasis on the primacy of pleasure sets it apart from other forms of art.

In this series of provocative and lucid essays Richard Dyer focuses on the genres most associated with entertainment, from musicals to action movies, disco to porn. He examines the nature of entertainment in movies such as *The Sound of Music* and *Speed*, and argues that entertainment is part of a common sense which is always historically and culturally constructed.

This new edition of *Only Entertainment* features a revised introduction and five new chapters on topics from serial killer movies to Elizabeth Taylor. In the final chapter Dyer asks whether entertainment as we know it is on the wane.

Richard Dyer is Professor of Film Studies at the University of Warwick. He is the author of *Now You See It: Studies in Lesbian and Gay Film* (1990), *The Matter of Images* (1993) and *White* (Routledge 1997).

ONLY ENTERTAINMENT

Second Edition

Richard Dyer

London and New York

First published 1992
by Routledge
2 Park Square, Milton Park, Abingdon, Oxon OX14 4RN

Simultaneously published in the USA and Canada
by Routledge
a division of Routledge, Chapman and Hall, Inc.
270 Madison Avenue, New York, NY 10016

Second edition published 2002

Routledge is an imprint of the Taylor & Francis Group

This edition published in the Taylor and Francis e-Library, 2005.

"To purchase your own copy of this or any of Taylor & Francis or Routledge's
collection of thousands of eBooks please go to www.eBookstore.tandf.co.uk."

British Library Cataloguing in Publication Data
A catalogue record for this book is available from the British Library

Library of Congress Cataloging-in-Publication Data
Dyer, Richard.
Only entertainment / Richard Dyer.–2nd ed.
p. cm
Includes bibliographical references and index.
1. Performing arts–Social aspects. 2. Popular culture. I. Title

PN1590.S6 D94 2002
306.4′84–dc21

2001058920

ISBN 0-203-99394-2 Master e-book ISBN

ISBN 0–415–25497–3 (pbk)
ISBN 0–415–25496–5 (hbk)

TO ROSALIND
FOR ALL THE RAINBOWS

CONTENTS

CONTENTS

ILLUSTRATIONS

1

INTRODUCTION

Entertainment is a guiding principle in the making and receiving of the arts and media. These essays address some of the meanings and implications of this.

Entertainment is an idea, one that is both historically and culturally specific. While pleasure has surely always been intended and taken in artefacts and performances, the idea of entertainment is distinctive in its emphasis on the primacy of such pleasure, ahead or even instead of practical, sacred, instructional or political aims and functions. This is touched on in chapters 2 and 5 ('The idea of entertainment', 'Entertainment and utopia'). Cultural developments since 1900 suggest that entertainment, at any rate in the forms discussed here, may also be historically specific in another sense, namely that it may now be on the way out, and this is addressed in a brief, speculative concluding essay, 'The waning of entertainment'.

The essays, written over a period of twenty-odd years and disparate in topic and tone, all seek to understand entertainment in its own terms. This means taking seriously the common sense of entertainment, notions like escapism, glamour, fun, stardom and excitement, as well as phrases such as 'it takes your mind off things' and 'it's only entertainment'. It also means analysing given instances of entertainment *as* entertainment, neither assuming one already understands what this is nor pushing the analysis too quickly on to other things. These are the effects of two other terms that have dominated discussion of entertainment: art and ideology.

The discourses of both art and ideology tend to take the idea of entertainment for granted, and therefore not to scrutinize it. The former either seeks to denigrate entertainment because it is not art (not formally perfect, accomplished or innovative, not emotionally deep, with nothing interesting to say about the world) or tries to show that such-and-such an instance of entertainment is really, or also, art; either way, the issue of what entertainment is is side-stepped. Discussion of ideology on the other hand tends to treat entertainment as a sugar on the pill of ideological messages, either condemning it as a disguise for world views of which the writer disapproves or else commending it as a strategy for promoting those of which she or he does approve. Once again, though, what entertainment is is not addressed.

1

If one uses the terms in a certain way, it is possible to consider all work of entertainment as also always works of art and ideology. They have formal properties and affects and perforce convey world views. In particular, one can try to show, as I do in these essays, how formal properties create, say, the élan of the musical, the allure of stars, the sensuality of disco or the excitement of action movies. However, to analyse entertainments in these terms is to refuse the in fact valuable evaluative connotations of art and ideology and only to consider the way form, affect and world view constitute the enjoyment that an entertainment proposes.

This does not mean that works of entertainment should be immune from ideological criticism. Indeed, one might define the project of these essays as the development of a political engagement with entertainment qua entertainment. This does fly in the face of one of the abiding beliefs of the discourse of entertainment, namely, that it is, after all, only entertainment. However any entertainment carries assumptions about and attitudes towards the world even if these are not the point of the thing; and the fact that an entertainment entertains does not let it off the hook of social responsibility, does not make up for sexism, racism or any other deleterious ism.

The task is to identify the ideological implications – good and bad – of entertainment qualities themselves, rather than seeking to uncover hidden ideological meanings behind and separable from the façade of entertainment. Thus in pointing, say, to the celebration of female energy and mastery of the world in *The Sound of Music*, I hope I have not just identified this as a politically welcome bonus alongside the lovely numbers but rather have shown it in what makes the numbers lovely: the force of Julie Andrews' delivery, the lilting drive of the tunes, the use of editing to display taking possession of the world. What I do not say in the essay on *The Sound of Music* but do in 'The colour of entertainment' and in relation to *Speed*, is that the very trope of mastery of the world – that gorgeous sense of sung, danced or 'actioned' expansion in space – also has negative ideological implications. The musical is unusual in assigning the experience of expansion to female characters, whereas *Speed* and action films generally are much more traditional in their gender division of entertainment labour; both however are part of a celebratory spreading out into and controlling of the world which has distinct racial and ecological implications. It is the feeling form of imperialism and the destruction of the planet. It is on such feelings and forms, the ends of entertainment, that ideological criticism focuses here rather than the ends to which entertainment may be put.

The topics discussed in these essays – which, if not exactly serendipitous, were certainly, and obviously, not chosen as part of a programme of research – are kinds of entertainment that few would dispute belong in the cultural category of entertainment: musicals, action movies, glamour stars, pin-ups, porn, dance music. Three depart slightly from this. Both ballet and the classic television serial are probably more readily perceived as belonging in

2

the category art rather than entertainment. My polemical intent with these brief pieces (and the references to the news as entertainment in 'Entertainment and utopia') is to unsettle the assumption that things that enjoy high cultural prestige are not in fact informed by the same entertainment values as those that are not – perhaps the former are just entertainment for highbrows. The other exception is the article on the trope of serial killing in, mainly, film and television. Here I have deliberately stressed both the formal enjoyments deployed in serial killing fictions (and by implication reportage), alongside the more usual address to its social significance, and also the moral and social significance of those enjoyments.

With these partial exceptions, the essays are about instances of entertainment provided by the industry and business principally responsible for the provision of entertainment. In other words, they are about the dominant definition of entertainment as carried in actual instances of entertainment. As a consequence, they do not ask, why do people like these things?, but rather, what ideas of being liked do these entertainments propose? what do these entertainments say entertainment is?

This collection was first published ten years ago.[1] It appeared in tandem with a collection of essays on representation (*The Matter of Images*). This volume sold considerably less well than *Images*. Perhaps the essays are simply not as good; certainly the cover wasn't. However I do also suspect that, amid all the current academic discussion of pleasure, desire, jouissance and carnival, entertainment is still not taken seriously as a topic. It is too social, too common-sensical, as likely conservative as progressive or transgressive; it is besides a solvent of taking things seriously. Representation obviously matters; entertainment is founded on not doing so. Yet any distinction between entertainment and representation is one of emphasis and convenience. Representation is a building block of things that are entertaining and the power of much representation resides in its ability to entertain.

Entertainment's representations have been especially concerned with temporarily providing, but also in the process defining, happiness. Goodness is more important than happiness, but only just and it is doubtful that we can be good without being happy (and vice versa). Politics is about fostering and maximizing happiness as well as goodness; we need constantly to have entertainment's ideas and experiences of what happiness might be and to reflect on them, their implications and costs. That is why it also matters to ask what entertainment is.

* * *

I should like to thank those who commissioned and encouraged these essays: Rebecca Barden, Rosalind Brunt, Jane Clarke, Philip Dodd, Jim Hillier, Ann Lloyd, Sally Townsend, Simon Watney and Christopher Williams. I also wish to acknowledge the following for stills and illustrations: BBC Photo Library

(Figure 4.1), BFI Stills, Posters and Designs (Figures 5.1, 5.2, 5.3, 5.4, 6.1 7.1, 7.2, 8.1, 8.2, 11.2, 11.3, 11.7, 11.8, 11.10, 12.1, 12.2, 12.3, 13.1 14.2, 14.3, 14.4, 17.1), Granada Television (Figure 4.2), MGM Ltd (Figure 14.1) and Playgirl Inc. (Figures 14.5, 14.10). Every effort has been made to obtain permission to reproduce copyright material. If any proper acknowl edgement has not been made we would invite copyright holders to inform us of the oversight.

Note

1   The articles on the colour of entertainment, *Speed*, serial killing and Elizabeth Taylor as well as the conclusion and this introduction, are additions to the 1992 edition the essay on camp in that edition is now to be found in my *The Culture of Queen* (London: Routledge, 2002).

Further reading

Bakhtin, Mikhail (1981) *Rabelais and His World*, Cambridge, MA: MIT Press.

Barthes, Roland (1975) *The Pleasure of the Text*, New York: Hill and Wang.

Barker, Martin and Brooks, Kate (1998) *Knowing Audiences: Judge Dredd, Its Friends, Far and Foes*, Luton: University of Luton Press.

Caughie, John (1986) 'Popular culture: notes and revisions', in MacCabe, Colin (ed *High Theory/Low Culture*, Manchester: Manchester University Press, 156–71.

Collins, Jim (1989) *Uncommon Cultures: Popular Culture and Post-modernism*, London Routledge.

Kracauer, Siegfried (1926) 'Kult der Zerstreuung', *Frankfurter Zeitung* 4 March; trans lated in *New German Critique* 40.

Lowenthal, Leo (1961) *Literature, Popular Culture and Society*, Englewood Cliffs, N_ Prentice-Hall.

Modleski, Tania (ed.) (1986) *Studies in Entertainment*, Bloomington, IN: Indian University Press.

Mulvey, Laura (1985) 'Visual pleasure and narrative cinema', in Nichols, Bill (ed.) *Movi and Methods*, Berkeley, CA: University of California Press, 305–15.

Rutsky, R. L. and Wyatt, Justin (1990) 'Serious pleasures: cinematic pleasure and th notion of fun', *Cinema Journal* 30 (1), 3–19.

Schlüpmann, Heide (1982) 'Kinosucht', *Frauen und Film* 33, 45–52.

Shiach, Morag (1989) *Discourse on Popular Culture: Class, Gender and History in Cultura Analysis, 1730 to the Present*, Oxford: Polity Press.

2

THE IDEA OF
ENTERTAINMENT

Uranie: [Molière] doesn't care if people attack his plays, as long
as plenty of people go to them.

*   *   *

Dorante: It's a skill, making people laugh.

*   *   *

Uranie: When I go to a show, I just consider the things that
move me, and if I've enjoyed myself, I don't start worrying about
whether I ought to have or whether Aristotle's rules forbid me to
laugh.

*   *   *

Dorante: Surely the rule of all rules is to please?
                   Molière: *The Critique of 'The School for Wives'*

The clown with his pants falling down,
Or the lights on the lady in tights,
Or the scene where the villain is mean,
   That's entertainment!
It might be a scene like you see on the screen,
A swain getting slain for the love of a queen,
Some great Shakespearean scene
Where a ghost and a prince meet
And everything ends in mincemeat.
    Howard Dietz and Arthur Schwartz: 'That's Entertainment!'

Entertainment, show business, Variety are not terms that are normally much
thought about. Indeed they are often the final point in a conversation: 'Well
anyway I like it. It's good entertainment', said defensively when you are
praising an unfashionable film in intellectual circles; or else the tag, now a
comic cliché, used in backstage musicals at crucial points in the plot: 'That's

5

show business!' Nothing more needs to be said: we all share a common-sense notion of what entertainment is. Yet precisely because it is such a final or absolute notion, it is very hard to define.

You can't get at it simply by listing examples. The song 'That's Entertainment!' by Dietz and Schwartz is a veritable compendium of what may be considered entertainment and lists, without any apparent sense of contradiction, *Hamlet* and *Oedipus Rex* alongside 'the clown with his pants falling down' and 'the lights on the lady in tights'. If all these things can be entertainment, then clearly entertainment is not so much a category of things as an attitude towards things.

We can best come to an understanding of what this attitude is by a series of negations.

First, entertainment is not simply a way of describing something found equally in all societies at all times. Song and dance in tribal societies, for instance, are specifically tied to religious and utilitarian purposes, placating the gods or conjuring up rain. The pageants and amusements of medieval Europe were part of the whole pattern of social life and built right into the organization of the calendar, governed by the Church and tied to seasonal – hence, economic – festivals. Where in tribal society song and dance sought to have an effect on life, in medieval society they celebrated it in a systematically structured way. Our entertainment may, of course, do both these things, but it is not in any coherent way associated with serious metaphysical or ceremonial practice. On the other hand, it is different from the growth of amusements and diversions in courtly society. Unlike them, modern entertainment is not simply a way of staving off days of boredom for a leisured class nor is it simply an adjunct to social intercourse.

A key figure in the emergence of 'entertainment' is Molière, who in having to elaborate a defence of his plays developed a new definition of what the theatre should do. The Church had attacked him for not edifying, the salons for his refusal to conform to the taste for polite *divertissement* and the critics for not obeying the rules of art. His defence was to deny that those concepts of what he should do were relevant to his real purpose, which was to provide pleasure – and the definition of *that* was to be decided by 'the people'. Against salons, Church and critics Molière set the court (which at this time was characterized by an impotent aristocracy and a newly recruited bourgeoisie who actually ran the country) and the gallery; against received élite opinion he asserted populism. In so doing, he severed art from entertainment – not, it is true, in his own practice but in theory. Entertainment became identified with what was not art, not serious, not refined. This distinction remains with us – art is what is edifying, élitist, refined, difficult, whilst entertainment is hedonistic, democratic, vulgar, easy. That the distinction is harmful, false to the best in both what is called art and what is called entertainment, has often been commented upon. But it remains one built into our education and, as we shall see, the decisions of television programmers.

Entertainment is also a part of 'leisure'. This is a specifically modern idea and is again best defined negatively, as is done, for instance, by Kenneth Roberts:

> Leisure time can be defined as time that is not obligated, and leisure activities can be defined as activities that are non-obligatory. At work, a man's time is not his own and his behaviour is not responsive purely to his own whims. Outside work, there are certain duties that men are obliged, either by custom or law, to fulfil, such as the obligations that an individual has towards his family. When these obligations have been met, a man has 'free time' in which his behaviour is dictated by his own will and preference, and it is here that leisure is found.
>
> (Roberts 1970: 6)

Leisure and entertainment are separate from and in opposition to work and domestic cares. In a functional analysis, leisure can be seen either as a way of compensating for the dreariness of work or else as the passivity attendant on industrial labour (cf. Wilensky 1962). But the richness and variety of the actual forms of leisure suggest that leisure should also be seen as the creation of meaning in a world in which work and the daily round are characterized by drudgery, insistence and meaninglessness.

Entertainment is a specific aspect of this leisure. It is provided and it is paid for, and in this it is unlike talking, hobbies, sex and games. It derives in its characteristic form – the string of short items with or without linkman, the popular and vulgar reference, the implicit sexuality and open sentimentality – from the development of entertainment in the pubs and clubs patronized by the urban working class.[1] This form has, of course, been fed by the continuing traditions of bourgeois amusement – operetta, musical comedy, parlour songs – but this has only tended to refine or embellish (and sometimes emasculate) the form, not to dominate it. Telescoping history in this way does, of course, miss out all sorts of nuance, but it does help us to grasp the specificity of the generalized contemporary notion, 'entertainment'.

If we now glance at a couple of official statements from BBC and ITV respectively we shall observe that this notion informs the thinking of these companies – not so much what they actually think or say, but what is implied in the sort of things they find it necessary to say publicly.

First, Tom Sloan's attempt to define light entertainment at a BBC lunchtime lecture:[2]

> We have Drama and Features and Arts Features and General Features and Documentaries *and* Talk and Current Affairs, to name but a few. But I believe that a great mass of people want to treat their television sets as a means of escape, and never more so than at the present time.

7

I remember one wet Sunday, in 1961, driving to Liverpool to see a new group called the Beatles give a concert for their fan club which we televised. For the first time in my life, I saw the industrial north of England, the rows of terraced houses, fronting on to the cobbled roads, glistening in the rain. The sheer ghastliness of it all was over-powering, but on the roof of every house, there was a television aerial. Antennae reaching for escape to another world. And, heaven knows, why not?

So my job is to organize a stream of output which is primarily intended to please and relax those who wish to receive it. In other words, to entertain.

As usual, we end up with that explain-all, 'to entertain', but before that we may note the careful distinction of entertainment from art and information and the distinction in terms of escape from the horrors of life. We should note, too, the rather patronizing tone of the man who provides entertainment for 'a great mass of people'. If we see entertainment from the point of view of the providers, then we are asking questions like, How do you distract people from the horrors of everyday life? What is strong enough to shut it out for a while? How do you bring a little sparkle into the drabness? and also How can you get on their side, not alienate them with art or education? This is the peculiar inflection of the responsible voice in mass entertainment and must have an influence on any aesthetic approach we make to it.

An ITV pronouncement[3] is equally revealing:

> It is common to write as though comedy and light entertainment were much the same thing. It is true that they have a common objective – to provide relaxing[4] entertainment. It is true, too, that in a country in which there are remnants of a puritan tradition the two are still sometimes lumped together as though they belonged in some rather disreputable bargain-basement of broadcasting. Nothing could be further from the truth. No aspect of broadcasting calls for greater skills or harder work from producers, directors and performers than the business of earning laughs or mounting an exciting production number.

Here there is an explicitly apologetic note, as is frequent enough in pronouncements from ITV, vulnerable to the attack of commercial exploitation. Their first answer, interestingly enough, is to defend the criticism of puritanism by a puritanical insistence on work, professionalism. This notion, however, is superseded in the next paragraph by even more powerful arguments

> There is still a shortage of light entertainment programmes of the highest quality. But it would be wrong to exaggerate. Many programmes have given a great deal of pleasure to very many people.

Populism has crept back, for the logic behind this is that as long as people enjoy it (or rather, as long as 'very many people' turn it on) it doesn't matter much what it's like.

Both these statements rely on a notion of entertainment such as has been sketched, but also reveal the peculiar quality of mass entertainment, provided by a specialist profession for people conceived of as an undifferentiated mass. Hence the philistinism and self-indulgence implicit in the notion are not tempered by the real vulgarity and consciousness of oppression of the people, but by the power of professional standards and the sensitivity of power to public opinion (both of which tend to temper vulgarity and indulgence in the name of responsibility) and more still by what producers think constitutes the entertainment needs of the working class.

Television light entertainment is founded on a very specific idea of what entertainment is in a modern industrial society. We must now look at the aesthetic consequences of this.[5]

from *Light Entertainment*, London: British Film Institute, 1973

Notes

1   A particularly interesting connection between the industrial experience and the actual form of entertainment is made in McLean 1965.
2   11 December 1969. Published as a pamphlet by the BBC.
3   *Independent Television Authority, Annual Report and Accounts, 1969–70*, London: HMSO, 15.
4   Note that both extracts use this word almost involuntarily. Its implication of prior tension links entertainment directly with the stresses of work and life.
5   The monograph from which this is taken *does* go on to look at the aesthetic consequences referred to above.

References

McLean, Albert F. Jr (1965) *American Vaudeville as Ritual*, Lexington, KY: University Press of Kentucky.
Roberts, Kenneth (1970) *Leisure*, London: Longman.
Wilensky, H. L. (1962) 'Labour and Leisure: intellectual traditions', *Industrial Relations* 1 (2).

3

A BIT OF UPLIFT

Classical ballet

The first time I saw Margot Fonteyn I was won over to classical ballet. I only ever saw her once live, from the very back of the next-to-highest level of Covent Garden. It was very hot and the stage was a very long way away. Rudolf Nureyev was in the show and seemed lazy and short on the anticipated smouldering sexuality. When Margot Fonteyn came on, I thought Here we go with all that fiddling and fussiness. Then with a simple gesture of her right arm, unfolding out from the elbow, I got the point. That gesture literally embodied grace, poise, elegance, and in a way that transformed those qualities from empty routines learnt by upper-class girls in finishing schools to a dream of living in harmony with one's body.

This quality is at the heart of George Balanchine's choreography for the New York City Ballet. Most of his ballets dispense with story-line and subject-matter while often using difficult contemporary music. They are often spoken about as 'pure' dance, which is fine if you mean they are not 'about' anything in a philosophical sense, but not if you mean they are not expressive. The interplay of the dancers that creates patterns of charm and beauty depends on coordination and interdependence, moments of unity and moments of harmonious contrast, a sense of what it is like to interact, collectively to create something. The ballets are not 'about' collectivity, but they do show it, and show how beautiful it could feel.

Going to evening classes to learn classical ballet convinced me of the value of ballet. In my mid-thirties, I was one of the oldest people there and for most of the time the only man. I was stiff and uncoordinated. It was potentially embarrassing and humiliating. In fact it was wonderful. For me it was a revelation that I could feel elegant and graceful in my body, that movement need not just be good for me because it made me fit and strong, but because it made me feel good about my body. For my fellow women pupils who had come, certainly, for the 'feminine' grace that classical ballet connotes, the exciting revelation was, on the contrary, precisely that feeling of stretch and strength in the muscles that is part of the pleasure of, for example, lifting weights.

Fonteyn, Balanchine, doing it – these are too inspiring, and too delightful, to be dismissed. Classical ballet celebrates the potential harmony of the human body, the utopian ideal of collective endeavour, the possibility of the interchange between the sexes of human qualities we now label masculine or feminine. Something of this is what has recommended ballet to the communisms of the USSR, Cuba and China. Beneath the aristocratic tat of the settings and the charming but dispensable never-never of the stories, there is an implicitly socialist vision.

Yet classical ballet must of course always come wrapped in the specifics of where and for whom it is performed, what other values and meanings it is attached to, and these are riven with contradictions. In practice, in Britain, classical ballet is, at one and the same time, élitist *and* popular, patriarchal *and* woman-centred, heterosexist *and* part of gay male culture, universal *and* distinctly white. It is all of this at once.

It is élitist in part because it is expensive. Not only are sets on a grand scale and not only do most of the classics require large casts, but behind all that there are the years of investment in training. Even a solo ballerina on a bare stage is the culmination of years of support and tuition. This élitism of money cuts two ways: those who get to be professional ballet dancers are the product of a rigorous process of selection; the high cost of putting on ballet means that there is not much of the live stuff about, to get in you have to be either wealthy or in the know. The symbol of classical ballet's élitism is Covent Garden, with its awe-inspiring entrance and studiedly dressed-down clientele, the usual story of the middle and upper classes nowadays getting reduced what they paid full price for before.

Yet classical ballet is also very popular. What live stuff there is is well attended. Figures for the six major dance companies (the Royal, Sadler's Wells, London Festival, Northern Rambert and London Contemporary) were well over a million during the past year [1985], despite the fact that cuts in subsidy mean there have actually been fewer performances. These figures do not take account of the numerous smaller companies, visiting companies and amateur performances. But this is only the tip of the iceberg of ballet's presence in our culture. Christmas TV always includes at least a couple of full-length ballets; pantomimes and Variety shows invariably include some kind of ballet spot (the good fairy is always in tutu and on point).

Above all, as a form of dance to learn, classical ballet remains a favourite. In local authority evening classes, it is the classical classes that you have to rush for to make sure you can get into them, even though there are far more such classes than in contemporary dance. The suburbs still have a generous quota of ballet schools aimed at little girls who still look alarmingly like miniature Margot Fonteyns.

These little girls are learning a dance form to which women have until recently been central. All the most interesting steps and roles, all the glory of the standard repertoire, is with the women. Yet it is male choreographers

11

who have designed these steps and roles and in the process have constructed an image of women as the epitome of delicacy, femininity at its most debilitating. Held aloft like feathers by the ballerinos, incarnating the souls of swans and sprites, billowing across the stage on tippy-toes – the image of women in classical ballet has often been decried in feminist analysis.

The reality of the production of this image is its own exact contrary – sinew and sweat, muscles and strength are the actual stock in trade of the female ballet dancer. There is often an emphasis in the coverage of men in ballet on how athletic it all is, how you have to be butch to be a male dancer. Fair enough, but so you do to be a female dancer. Classical ballet has been one of the few areas, until very recently, where women were encouraged indeed required, to develop their muscles, stamina and power, yet all in the service of the opposite feminine ideal.

The image of woman as sprite is of a piece with the way classical ballet focuses on the perfect heterosexual couple. Why then the gay appeal? One cannot reduce the appeal of something to a particular audience to one factor alone. Some gay men have been balletomanes for everything from the fact of ballet's extreme escapism from an uncongenial world to its display of the male physique, and to its reputation as an area of employment in which gay men could be open and safe.

There is also something about ballet's image of heterosexuality that fits with other items popular in gay male circles. Heterosexuality in classical ballet is so extreme, so refined, so ethereally idealized that it becomes rather unreal, a chimera. In a camp appreciation, this means enjoying the spectacle of heterosexuality paraded as glittering illusion. In a more aestheticized appreciation, the very abstraction of love in ballet renders it a kind of essence, not about women and men, nor about real people even, but the embodiment of an idea of human relationships that anyone can relate to.

Classical ballet yearns towards the potentials of the human body, all human bodies, stripped of the specifics of class, gender and sexuality. Yet there is also something distinctly white about ballet in Great Britain. In the USA many of the top classical dancers are black, but not here. Perhaps this has been due to recruitment problems in the past. It is only recently that black dance groups, having found a new confidence in black traditions of dance, are turning to classical technique to extend their range. Yet there is also racism among balletomanes. There lingers a view of the 'primitivism' of black people and their cultural traditions which is at odds with the idea of poise and elegance so prized in classical ballet. But, if we look to the US traditions, we can see how the involvement of black dancers has enriched and inflected the classical image so that it becomes an affirmation of the way that, racially speaking, all kinds of body are graceful and powerful, vital and beautiful.

No art is truly universal, truly all-inclusive. Ballet does not accommodate disabled bodies and, as performers though not as participants, is unlikely to celebrate old or fat bodies. At one level, its yearning for the transcendent grace of the individual human body in the abstract is a refusal of the actual limitations of the human body in reality. But at another level, its dream of being at one with one's body and of being in harmony (united in and through differences) with other bodies is the feeling form of socialism. And the fact that you have to train and work for this is what makes it most powerful of all. Classical ballet does not say harmony is natural to human beings, but rather that we can learn to achieve it. Likewise, socialism does not emanate from us naturally, it is the harmony we can learn to create together.

Marxism Today, January 1986

Further reading

Daly, Ann (1987) 'The Balanchine woman', *The Drama Review* 113: 8–21.

Kealiinohomoku, Joann (1983) 'An anthropologist looks at ballet as a form of ethnic dance', in Roger Copeland and Selma Jean Cohen (eds) *What is Dance?*, Oxford: Oxford University Press.

McRobbie, Angela (1990) '*Fame, Flashdance* and fantasies of achievement', in Jane Gaines and Charlotte Herzog (eds) *Fabrications: Costume and the Female Body*, New York and London: Routledge, 3–58.

4

QUALITY PLEASURES

Rupert Murdoch putting the knife into 'quality drama' at the Edinburgh Television Festival is a bit of an embarrassment.[1] 'Qualities' have long been the bogeys of left criticism, their emotional restraint and good taste the embodiment of a middle-class, middle-aged, suburban sensibility, their period detail the televisual equivalent of the heritage industry, their over-riding tones of regret and disappointment expended on the days of empire, classes in their place and servants always obtainable. It may not be Thatcherite television, too sad, uncertain and backward-looking for that, but it does com-fort the middle classes with the proposition that however nice their homes and clothes, they do suffer a lot and it's hard to know anyway what's right and what's wrong, everything is so nuanced and 'difficult'.

Qualities are often both snobbish and complacent. The knee-jerk approval they get from so many within the industry and from television critics is so insufferable that one could almost be grateful for Mr Murdoch's spade-calling, were it not for one's awareness of the incommensurably greater tide of snobbery and complacency in his empire. One of the problems of the knee-jerk approval ('the British do these things so well') is that it is usually couched in terms of the qualities being somehow better than other things on tele-vision. They are not, necessarily. They have their own pleasures, which are their own justification.

The idea that the qualities are supremely 'well done' does not really tell you what they are doing. The phrase echoes those characters in Barbara Pym novels who observe wistfully of women a little better off than they that what these women wear may not look much but is 'good'. The well-done-ness has to do with the provenance of the material, the attention to detail and finish in acting, costume and setting, and the slowish pace, where aspects of how the thing is done take precedence over rattling through the plot or cele-brating vivid performance. There is a thickness of texture in the qualities, very different from most soaps or US teledramas, where milieu and income are signalled through the selection of a few opulently designed or highly suggestive items of dress and décor.

The pleasure of this well-done density is partly sensuous – *Fortunes of War* would have been worth it for Harriet's cardigans and tea-cups alone (Figure 4.1); or, as a friend of mine puts it, the only trouble with qualities is that the actors will keep standing in front of the furniture. It is sensuousness in a particular register. Although the qualities are undoubtedly very expensive, and most viewers know it, they are rarely set in worlds of the most extravagant or fashionable luxury. While most people could not afford to live as the characters in qualities do, it is just about possible to imagine being able to. Moreover, the detail and finish provide a pleasure akin to that taken by all enthusiasts of crafts, not least ones widely practised like carpentry, knitting, cooking, gardening. There is a relish and delight to be had from recognizing the skill and care that go into the qualities.

All of this well-done sensuousness is lavished on characters, settings and situations that are overridingly domestic and local. Qualities are therefore sometimes characterized, pejoratively, as 'superior soaps'. There would be nothing wrong with them if this were so (whatever it means), but in fact it misses what is specific to them.

In the qualities there are two countervailing tendencies. On the one hand, there is a strong feeling that the characters and what is happening to them are not really where it's at, a feeling of which they are often acutely aware. There are often offscreen, as crucial reference points, momentous world-historical events taking place: the end of the British Empire in India, the rise of fascism and the Second World War, the growth and decline of the welfare state in Britain, and so on. The characters, especially but not only the women, are aware of what's going on, but feel unable to affect or comprehend it – hence the mood of bafflement and melancholy, the strong sense of stasis rather than dynamic plot development. Nothing could be more unlike soap operas. With them, home and community are where it's at, plots are squandered with astounding largesse. There may be recognition of 'wider' realms and events, but they are marginal to the real business of family, friends, day-to-day life. Soaps and the qualities may both favour the domestic, local world – the world of affect – but for the former that is also the centre of the world at large whereas for the qualities it is the margin.

On the other hand, the wider world does suddenly, distressingly, erupt into these margins. Wartime settings achieve this with the greatest of ease: arbitrary, unforeseeable, often gruesome deaths and maimings interrupt the round of perplexed marginality. This does not pull the characters to the centre of the world – it shatters the cosy safety of their lives while still reinforcing that sense of confusion and helplessness that is the qualities' abiding one.

Soaps affirm and validate the importance of the immediate and the everyday, while the qualities give recognition to another, surely equally widespread, feeling of events, decisions, power going on elsewhere, over there, beyond our control or comprehension, though not so far beyond as to be

Figure 4.1 Fortunes of War: Harriet and cardigan

Figure 4.2 The Jewel in the Crown: awkwardness in empire

incapable of hurting us. Both such constructions of feeling have their appeals, their strengths and limitations. One is not better than another; both discourage any sense of or desire for empowerment in the worlds of work, politics and 'society'; both validate different notions of the place of the domestic and local in the world. We do not need to defend one (qualities and public service broadcasting) at the critical expense of the other (soaps and monopolized, deregulated broadcasting). It is clear, however, that public service broadcasting has a better record at providing both. Certainly compared to Mr Murdoch.

New Statesman and Society, July 1989

Note

1   In 1989 Rupert Murdoch, the owner of huge private press and broadcasting systems, gave a keynote speech at the Edinburgh International Television Festival addressing the current debate over public broadcasting and castigating the latter's defenders for élitist championing of documentary and literary adaptations. This occasioned the commissioning of this article.

Further reading

Brunsdon, Charlotte (1990) 'Problems with quality', *Screen* 31 (1): 67–90.

Caughie, John (2000) 'Small pleasures: adaptation and the past in the classic serial' in *Television Drama: Realism, Modernism and British Culture*, Oxford: Oxford University Press, 203–25.

Geraghty, Christine (1991) *Women and Soap Opera*, Cambridge: Polity Press.

Wollen, Tana (1991) 'Over our shoulders: nostalgic screen fictions for the 1980s', in John Corner and Sylvia Harvey (eds) *Enterprise and Heritage: Crosscurrents of National Culture*, London, Routledge, 178–93.

5

ENTERTAINMENT
AND UTOPIA

This article is about musicals as entertainment. I don't necessarily want to
disagree with those who would claim that musicals are also 'something else'
(e.g. 'Art') or argue that entertainment itself is only a product of 'something
more important' (e.g. political/economic manipulation, psychological forces),
but I want to put the emphasis here on entertainment as entertainment.
Musicals were predominantly conceived of, by producers and audiences alike,
as 'pure entertainment' – the *idea* of entertainment was a prime determinant
on them. Yet because entertainment is a common-sense, 'obvious' idea, what
is really meant and implied by it never gets discussed.

Musicals are one of a whole string of forms – music hall, variety, TV spec-
taculars, pantomime, cabaret, etc. – that are usually summed up by the term
'showbiz'. The idea of entertainment I want to examine here is most centrally
embodied by these forms, although I believe that it can also be seen at work,
mutatis mutandis, in other forms and I suggest below, informally, how this
might be so. However, it is probably true to, say that 'showbiz' is the most
thoroughly entertainment-oriented of all types of performance, and that
notions of myth, art, instruction, dream and ritual may be equally important, even at the conscious level, with regard to, say, Westerns, the news,
soap opera, or rock music.

It is important, I think, to stress the cultural and historical specificity of
entertainment. The kinds of performance produced by professional entertainment are different in audience, performers and above all intention to the
kinds of performance produced in tribal, feudal, or socialist societies. It is
not possible here to provide the detailed historical and anthropological argument to back this up, but I hope the differences will suggest themselves
when I say that entertainment is a type of performance produced for profit,
performed before a generalized audience (the 'public'), by a trained, paid
group who do nothing else but produce performances which have the sole
(conscious) aim of providing pleasure.

Because entertainment is produced by professional entertainers, it is also
largely defined by them. That is to say, although entertainment is part of
the coinage of everyday thought, none the less how it is defined, what it is

assumed to be, is basically decided by those people responsible (paid) for providing it in concrete form. Professional entertainment is the dominant agency for defining what entertainment is. This does not mean, however, that it *simply* reproduces and expresses patriarchal capitalism. There is the usual struggle between capital (the backers) and labour (the performers) over control of the product, and professional entertainment is unusual in that: (1) it is in the business of producing forms not things, and (2) the workforce (the performers themselves) is in a better position to determine the form of its product than are, say, secretaries or car workers. The fact that professional entertainment has been by and large conservative in this century should not blind us to the implicit struggle within it, and looking beyond class to divisions of sex and race, we should note the important role of structurally subordinate groups in society – women, blacks, gays – in the development and definition of entertainment. In other words, show business's relationship to the demands of patriarchal capitalism is a complex one. Just as it does not simply 'give the people what they want' (since it actually defines those wants), so, as a relatively autonomous mode of cultural production, it does not simply reproduce unproblematically patriarchal-capitalist ideology. Indeed, it is precisely on seeming to achieve both these often opposed functions simultaneously that its survival largely depends.

Two of the taken-for-granted descriptions of entertainment, as 'escape' and as 'wish-fulfilment', point to its central thrust, namely, utopianism. Entertainment offers the image of 'something better' to escape into, or something we want deeply that our day-to-day lives don't provide. Alternatives, hopes, wishes – these are the stuff of utopia, the sense that things could be better, that something other than what is can be imagined and maybe realized.

Entertainment does not, however, present models of utopian worlds, as in the classic utopias of Thomas More, William Morris, *et al.* Rather the utopianism is contained in the feelings it embodies. It presents, head-on as it were, what utopia would feel like rather than how it would be organized. It thus works at the level of sensibility, by which I mean an affective code that is characteristic of, and largely specific to, a given mode of cultural production.

This code uses both representational and, importantly, non-representational signs. There is a tendency to concentrate on the former, and clearly it would be wrong to overlook them – stars are nicer than we are, characters more straightforward than people we know, situations more soluble than those we encounter. All this we recognize through representational signs. But we also recognize qualities in non-representational signs – colour, texture, movement, rhythm, melody, camerawork – although we are much less used to talking about them.

The nature of non-representational signs is not, however, so different from that of representational. Both are, in Peirce's terminology, largely iconic but whereas the relationship between signifier and signified in a representational icon is one of resemblance between their appearance, their look, the relationship in the case of the non-representational icon is one of resemblance at the level of basic structuration.

This concept has been developed (among other places) in the work of Susanne K. Langer, particularly in relation to music. We are moved by music, yet it has the least obvious reference to 'reality' – the intensity of our response to it can only be accounted for by the way music, abstract, formal though it is, still embodies feeling.

> The tonal structures we call 'music' bear a close logical similarity to the forms of human feeling – forms of growth and of attenuation, flowing and stowing, conflict and resolution, speed, arrest, terrific excitement, calm or subtle activation or dreamy lapses – not joy and sorrow perhaps, but the poignancy of both – the greatness and brevity and eternal passing of everything vitally felt. Such is the pattern, or logical form, of sentience; and the pattern of music is that same form worked out in pure measures, sound and silence. Music is a tonal analogue of emotive life.
>
> Such formal analogy, or congruence of logical structures, is the prime requisite for the relation between a symbol and whatever it is to mean. The symbol and the object symbolized must have some common logical form.
>
> (Langer 1953: 27)

Langer realizes that recognition of a common logical form between a performance sign and what it signifies is not always easy or natural: 'The congruence of two given perceptible forms is not always evident upon simple inspection. The common *logical* form they both exhibit may become apparent only when you know the principle whereby to relate them' (ibid.). This implies that responding to a performance is not spontaneous – you have to learn what emotion is embodied before you can respond to it. A problem with this as Langer develops it is the implication that the emotion itself is not coded, is simply 'human feeling'. I would be inclined, however, to see almost as much coding in the emotions as in the signs for them. Thus, just as writers such as E. H. Gombrich and Umberto Eco stress that different modes of representation (in history and culture) correspond to different modes of perception, so it is important to grasp that modes of experiential art and entertainment correspond to different culturally and historically determined sensibilities.

This becomes clear when one examines how entertainment forms come to have the emotional signification they do: that is, by acquiring their signification in relation to the complex of meanings in the social-cultural situation in which they are produced. Take the extremely complex history of tap dance – in black culture, tap dance has had an improvisatory, self-expressive

Table 5.1

	Energy	*Abundance*
	Capacity to act vigorously; human power, activity, potential	Conquest of scarcity; having enough to spare without sense of poverty of others; enjoyment of sensuous material reality
Show-biz forms	Dance – tap, Latin-American, American Theater Ballet; also 'oomph', 'pow', 'pizazz' qualities of performance	Spectacle; Ziegfeld, Busby Berkeley, MGM
Sources of show-biz forms	Tap – black and white folk culture; American Theater Ballet – modern dance plus folk dance plus classical ballet	Court displays; high art influences on Ziegfeld, Cedric Gibbons (MGM); *haute couture*
Golddiggers of 1933	'Pettin' in the Park' (tap, roller skates; quick tempo at which events are strung together)	'Pettin' . . .' (leisure park) 'We're in the Money' (showgirls dressed in coins) 'Shadow Waltz' (lavish sets; tactile, non-functional, wasteful clothing; violins as icon of high culture, i.e. expense)
Funny Face	'Think Pink' 'Clap Yo' Hands' (tap) 'Let's Kiss and Make Up' (tap, and Astaire's longevity) Cellar dance	'Think Pink' (use of materials and fabrics) 'Bonjour Paris' 'On How to be Lovely' (creation of fashion image)
On the Town	'New York, New York' 'On the Town' 'Prehistoric Man' 'Come Up to My Place'	'New York, New York' (cf. 'Bonjour Paris') 'Miss Turnstiles' (woman as commodity-fantasy)
Westerns	Chases, fights, bar-room brawls; pounding music (1960s onwards)	Land – boundlessness and/or fertility
TV news	Speed of series of sharp, short items; the 'latest' news; hand-held camera	Technology of news-gathering – satellites, etc.; doings of rich; spectacles of pageantry and destruction

Table 5.1 (cont.)

Intensity	Transparency	Community
Experiencing of emotion directly, fully, unambiguously, 'authentically', without holding back	A quality of relationships – between represented characters (e.g. true love), between performer and audience ('sincerity')	Togetherness, sense of belonging, network of phatic relationships (i.e. those in which communication is for its own sake rather than for its message)
'Incandescent' star performers (Garland, Bassey, Streisand); torch singing	'Sincere' stars (Crosby, Gracie Fields); love and romance	The singalong chorus numbers
Star phenomenon in wider society; the Blues	Star phenomenon in wider society; eighteenth-century sentimental novel	Pub entertainment *and* parlour balladry; choral traditions in folk and church
'Forgotten Man' 'I've Got to Sing a Torch Song' (Blues inflections)	'Shadow Waltz' (Keeler and Powell as couple in eye-to-eye contact).	Showgirls (wisecracking interaction, mutual support – e.g. sharing clothes)
How Long Has This Been Going On?'	'Funny Face' 'He Loves and She Loves' ''S Wonderful'	(?) Cellar dance
'A Day in New York' ballet; climactic chase	'You're Awful' (insult turned into declaration of love) 'Come up to My Place' (direct invitation)	'You Can Count on Me'
Confrontation on street; suspense	Cowboy as 'man' – straight, straightforward, morally unambiguous, puts actions where his words are	Townships; cowboy camaraderie
Emphasis on violence, dramatic incident; selection of visuals with eye to climactic moments	(?) 'Man of the people' manner of some newscasters, celebrities and politicians (?) simplification of events to allow easy comprehension	The world rendered as global village; assumptions of consensus

function similar to that in jazz; in minstrelsy, it took on an aspect of jolly mindlessness, inane good humour, in accord with minstrelsy's image of the Negro; in vaudeville, elements of mechanical skill, tap dance as a feat, were stressed as part of vaudeville's celebration of the machine and the brilliant performer. Clearly there are connections between these different significations, and there are residues of all of them in tap as used in films, television and contemporary theatre shows. This has little to do, however, with the intrinsic meanings of hard, short, percussive, syncopated sounds arranged in patterns and produced by the movement of feet, and everything to do with the significance such sounds acquire from their place within the network of signs in a given culture at a given point of time. Nevertheless, the signification is essentially apprehended through the coded non-representational form (although the representational elements usually present in a performance sign – a dancer is always 'a person dancing' – may help to anchor the necessarily more fluid signification of the non-representational elements; for example, a black man, a white man in blackface, a troupe, or a white woman tap-dancing may suggest different ways of reading the taps, because each relates to a slightly different moment in the evolution of the non-representational form, tap dance).

I have laboured this point at greater length than may seem warranted partly with polemic intent. First, it seems to me that the reading of non-representational signs in the cinema is particularly undeveloped. On the one hand, the *mise-en-scène* approach (at least as classically developed in *Movie* tends to treat the non-representational as a function of the representational simply a way of bringing out, emphasizing, aspects of plot, character, situation, without signification in their own right. On the other hand, semiotics has been concerned with the codification of the representational. Second, I feel that film analysis remains notoriously non-historical, except in rather lumbering, simplistic ways. My adaptation of Langer seeks to emphasize not the connection between signs and historical events, personages, or forces, but rather the history of signs themselves as they are produced in culture and history. Nowhere here has it been possible to reproduce the detail of any sign's history (and I admit to speculation in some instances), but most of the assertions are based on more thorough research, and even where they are not, they should be.

The categories of entertainment's utopian sensibility are sketched in the accompanying Table 5.1, together with examples of them. The three films used will be discussed below; the examples from Westerns and television news are just to suggest how the categories may have wider application; the sources referred to are the cultural, historical situation of the code's production.

The categories are, I hope, clear enough, but a little more needs to be said about 'intensity'. It is hard to find a word that quite gets what I mean. What

I have in mind is the capacity of entertainment to present either complex or unpleasant feelings (e.g. involvement in personal or political events; jealousy, loss of love, defeat) in a way that makes them seem uncomplicated, direct and vivid, not 'qualified' or 'ambiguous' as day-to-day life makes them, and without intimations of self-deception and pretence. (Both intensity and transparency can be related to wider themes in the culture, as 'authenticity' and 'sincerity' respectively – see Trilling 1972.)

The obvious problem raised by this breakdown of the utopian sensibility is where these categories come from. One answer, at a very broad level, might be that they are a continuation of the utopian tradition in western thought. George Kateb describes what he takes to be the dominant motifs in this tradition, and they do broadly overlap with those outlined above. Thus:

> when a man [sic] thinks of perfection . . . he thinks of a world permanently without strife, poverty, constraint, stultifying labour, irrational authority, sensual deprivation . . . peace, abundance, leisure, equality, consonance of men and their environment.
>
> (1972: 9)

We may agree that notions in this broad conceptual area are common throughout western thought, giving it, and its history, its characteristic dynamic, its sense of moving beyond what is to what ought to be or what we want to be. However, the very broadness, and looseness, of this common ground does not get us very far – we need to examine the specificity of entertainment's utopia.

One way of doing so is to see the categories of the sensibility as temporary answers to the inadequacies of the society which is being escaped from through entertainment. This is proposed by Hans Magnus Enzensberger in his 'Constituents of a theory of the media'. He takes issue with the traditional left-wing use of concepts of 'manipulation' and 'false needs' in relation to the mass media:

> The electronic media do not owe their irresistible power to any sleight-of-hand but to the elemental power of deep social needs which come through even in the present depraved form of these media.
>
> (1972: 113)

> Consumption as spectacle contains the promise that want will disappear. The deceptive, brutal and obscene features of this festival derive from the fact that there can be no question of a real fulfilment of its promise. But so long as scarcity holds sway, use-value remains a decisive category which can only be abolished by trickery. Yet trickery on such a scale is only conceivable if it is based on mass need. This need – it is a utopian one – is there. It is the desire for

25

Table 5.2

Social tension/inadequacy/absence	Utopian solution
Scarcity (actual poverty in the society; poverty observable in the surrounding societies, e.g. Third World); unequal distribution of wealth	Abundance (elimination of poverty for self and others; equal distribution of wealth)
Exhaustion (work as a grind, alienated labour, pressures of urban life)	Energy (work and play synonymous), city-dominated (*On the Town*) or pastoral return (*The Sound of Music*)
Dreariness (monotony, predictability, instrumentality of the daily round)	Intensity (excitement, drama, affectivity of living)
Manipulation (advertising, bourgeois democracy, sex roles)	Transparency (open, spontaneous, honest communications and relationships)
Fragmentation (job mobility, rehousing and development, high-rise flats, legislation against collective action)	Community (all together in one place, communal interests, collective activity)

a new ecology, for a breaking-down of environmental barriers, for an aesthetic which is not limited to the sphere of the 'artistic'. These desires are not – or are not primarily – internalized rules of the games as played by the capitalist system. They have physiological roots and can no longer be suppressed. Consumption as spectacle is – in parody form – the anticipation of a utopian situation.

(ibid.: 114)

This does, I think, express well the complexity of the situation. However, Enzensberger's appeal to 'elemental' and 'physiological' demands, although we do not need to be too frightened by them, is lacking in both historical and anthropological perspectives. I would rather suggest, a little over-schematically, that the categories of the utopian sensibility are related to specific inadequacies in society. I illustrate this in Table 5.2.

The advantage of this analysis is that it does offer some explanation of why entertainment *works*. It is not just leftovers from history, it is not *just* what show business, or 'they', force on the rest of us, it is not simply the expression of eternal needs – it responds to real needs *created by society*. The weakness of the analysis (and this holds true for Enzensberger too) is in the give-away absences from the left-hand column – no mention of class, race, or patriarchy. That is, while entertainment is responding to needs that are real, at the same time it is also defining and delimiting what constitute the legitimate needs of people in this society.

I am not trying to recoup here the false needs argument – we are talking about real needs created by real inadequacies, but they are not the only needs and inadequacies of the society. Yet entertainment, by so orienting itself to them, effectively denies the legitimacy of other needs and inadequacies, and especially of class, patriarchal and sexual struggles. (Though once again we have to admit the complexity and contradictions of the situation – that, for instance, entertainment is not the only agency which defines legitimate needs, and that the actual role of women, gay men and blacks in the creation of show business leaves its mark in such central oppositional icons as, respectively, the strong woman type, e.g. Ethel Merman, Judy Garland, Elsie Tanner, camp humour and sensuous taste in dress and decor, and almost all aspects of dance and music. Class, it will be noted, is still nowhere.)

Class, race and sexual caste are denied validity as problems by the dominant (bourgeois, white, male) ideology of society. We should not expect show business to be markedly different. However, there is one further turn of the screw, and that is that, with the exception perhaps of community (the most directly working-class in source), the ideals of entertainment imply wants that capitalism itself promises to meet. Thus abundance becomes consumerism, energy and intensity personal freedom and individualism, and transparency freedom of speech. In other (Marcuse's) words, it is a partially 'one-dimensional' situation. The categories of the sensibility point to gaps or inadequacies in capitalism, but only those gaps or inadequacies that capitalism proposes itself to deal with. At our worse sense of it, entertainment provides alternatives *to* capitalism which will be provided *by* capitalism.

However, this one-dimensionality is seldom so hermetic, because of the deeply contradictory nature of entertainment forms. In Variety, the essential contradiction is between comedy and music turns; in musicals, it is between the narrative and the numbers. Both these contradictions can be rendered as one between the heavily representational and verisimilitudinous (pointing to the way the world is, drawing on the audience's concrete experience of the world) and the heavily non-representational and 'unreal' (pointing to how things could be better). In musicals, contradiction is also to be found at two other levels – within numbers, between the representational and the non-representational, and within the non-representational, due to the differing sources of production inscribed in the signs.

To be effective, the utopian sensibility has to take off from the real experiences of the audience. Yet to do this, to draw attention to the gap between what is and what could be, is, ideologically speaking, playing with fire. What musicals have to do, then, (not through any conspiratorial intent, but because it is always easier to take the line of least resistance, i.e. to fit in with prevailing norms) is to work through these contradictions at all levels in such a way as to 'manage' them, to make them seem to disappear. They don't always succeed.

27

I have chosen three musicals (*Golddiggers of 1933, Funny Face, On the Town* which seem to me to illustrate the three broad tendencies of musicals – those that keep narrative and number clearly separated (most typically, the back stage musical); those that retain the division between narrative as problem and numbers as escape, but try to 'integrate' the numbers by a whole set of papering-over-the-cracks devices (e.g. the well-known 'cue for a song'); and those which try to dissolve the distinction between narrative and numbers thus implying that the world of the narrative is also (already) utopian.

The clear separation of numbers and narrative in *Golddiggers of 1933* is broadly in line with a 'realist' aesthetic: the numbers occur in the film in the same way as they occur in life, that is, on stages and in cabarets. This 'realism' is of course reinforced by the social-realist orientation of the narrative, setting and characterization, with their emphasis on the Depression, poverty, the quest for capital, 'golddigging' (and prostitution). However, the numbers are not wholly contained by this realist aesthetic – the way in which they are opened out, in scale and in cinematic treatment (overhead shots, etc. represents a quite marked shift from the real to the non-real, and from the largely representational to the largely non-representational (sometimes to the point of almost complete abstraction) (Figure 5.1). The thrust of the narrative is towards seeing the show as a 'solution' to the personal Depression-induced problems of the characters; yet the non-realist presentation of the numbers makes it very hard to take this solution seriously. It is 'just' escape, 'merely' utopian.

If the numbers embody (capitalist) palliatives to the problems of the narrative – chiefly, abundance (spectacle) in place of poverty, and (non-efficacious) energy (chorines in self-enclosed patterns) in place of dispiritedness – then the actual mode of presentation undercuts this by denying it the validity of 'realism'.

However, if one then looks at the contradiction between the representational and non-representational within the numbers, this becomes less clear-cut. Here much of the representational level reprises the lessons of the narrative – above all, that women's only capital is their bodies as objects. The abundant scale of the numbers is an abundance of piles of women; the sensuous materialism is the texture of femaleness; the energy of the dancing (when it occurs) is the energy of the choreographic imagination, to which the dancers are subservient. Thus, while the non-representational certainly suggests an alternative to the narrative, the representational merely reinforces the narrative (women as sexual coinage, women – and men – as expression of the male producer).

Finally, if one then looks at the non-representational alone, contradictions once again become apparent – e.g. spectacle as materialism and metaphysic (that is, on the one hand, the sets, costumes, etc., are tactile, sensuous, physically exhilarating, but on the other hand, are associated with fairyland

Figure 5.1 Women as abundance: *Golddiggers of 1933*

magic, the by-definition immaterial), dance as human creative energy *and* subhuman mindlessness.

In *Funny Face*, the central contradiction is between art and entertainment, and this is further worked through in the antagonism between the central couple, Audrey Hepburn (art) and Fred Astaire (entertainment). The numbers are escapes from the problems, and discomforts, of the contradiction – either by asserting the unanswerably more pleasurable qualities of entertainment (e.g. 'Clap Yo' Hands' following the dirge-like Juliette Greco-type song in the 'empathicalist', i.e. existentialist, *soirée*), or in the transparency of love in the Hepburn–Astaire numbers.

But it is not always that neat. In the empathicalist cellar club, Hepburn escapes Astaire in a number with some of the other beats in the club. This reverses the escape direction of the rest of the film (i.e. it is an escape from entertainment/Astaire into art). Yet within the number, the contradiction repeats itself. Before Hepburn joins the group, they are dancing in a style deriving from Modern Dance, angular, oppositional shapes redolent in musical convention of neurosis and pretentiousness (cf. Danny Kaye's number, 'Choreography', in *White Christmas*). As the number proceeds, however more showbiz elements are introduced – use of syncopated clapping, forming in a vaudeville line-up, and American Theater Ballet shapes. Here an 'art' form is taken over and infused with the values of entertainment. This is a contradiction between the representational (the dreary night club) and the non-representational (the oomph of music and movement), but also within the non-representational, between different dance forms. The contradiction between art and entertainment is thus repeated at each level.

In the love numbers, too, contradictions appear, partly by the continuation in them of troubling representational elements. In 'Funny Face', photographs of Hepburn as seen by Astaire, the fashion photographer, are projected on the wall as background to his wooing her and her giving in. Again, their final dance of reconciliation to ''S Wonderful' takes place in the grounds of a château, beneath the trees, with doves fluttering around them (Figure 5.2). Earlier, this setting was used as the finish for their fashion photography sequence. In other words, in both cases, she is reconciled to him only by capitulating to his definition of her (Figure 5.3). In itself, there is nothing contradictory in this – it is what Ginger Rogers always had to do. But here the mode of reconciliation is transparency and yet we can see the strings of the number being pulled. Thus the representational elements, which bespeak manipulation of romance, contradict the non-representational, which bespeak its transparency.

The two tendencies just discussed are far more common than the third, which has to suggest that utopia is implicit in the world of the narrative as well as in the world of the numbers.

The commonest procedure for doing this is removal of the whole film in time and space – to turn-of-the-century America (*Meet Me in St Louis, Hello Dolly!*), Europe (*The Merry Widow, Gigi, Song of Norway*), cockney London (*My Fair Lady, Oliver!, Scrooge*), black communities (*Hallelujah!, Cabin in the Sky, Porgy and Bess*), etc. – to places, that is, where it can be believed (by white urban Americans) that song and dance are 'in the air', built into the peasant/black culture and blood, or part of a more free-and-easy stage in American development. In these films, the introduction of any real narrative concerns is usually considerably delayed and comes chiefly as a temporary threat to utopia – thus reversing the other two patterns, where the narrative predominates and numbers function as temporary escapes from it. Not much happens, plot-wise, in *Meet Me in St Louis* until we have had 'Meet Me in St Louis', 'The Boy Next Door' 'The Trolley Song' and 'Skip to My Lou' – only then does father come along with his proposal to dismantle this utopia by his job mobility.

Most of the contradictions developed in these films are overridingly bought off by the nostalgia or primitivism which provides them with the point of departure. Far from pointing forwards, they point back, to a golden age – a reversal of utopianism that is only marginally offset by the narrative motive of recovery of utopia. What makes *On the Town* interesting is that its utopia is a well-known modern city. The film starts as an escape – from the confines of navy life into the freedom of New York, and also from the weariness of work, embodied in the docker's refrain, 'I feel like I'm not out of bed yet', into the energy of leisure, as the sailors leap into the city for their day off. This energy runs through the whole film, *including the narrative*. In most musicals, the narrative represents things as they are, to be escaped from. But most of the narrative of *On the Town* is about the transformation of New York into utopia. The sailors release the *social* frustrations of the women – a tired taxi driver just coming off shift, a hard-up dancer reduced to belly-dancing to pay for ballet lessons, a woman with a sexual appetite that is deemed improper – not so much through love and sex as through energy. This sense of the sailors as a transforming energy is heightened by the sense of pressure on the narrative movement suggested by the device of a time-check flashed on the screen intermittently.

This gives a historical dimension to a musical, that is, it shows people making utopia rather than just showing them from time to time finding themselves in it. But the people are men – it is still men making history, not men and women together. And the Lucy Schmeeler role is unforgivably male chauvinist. In this context, the 'Prehistoric Man' number is particularly interesting (Figure 5.4). It centres on Ann Miller, and she leads the others in the takeover of the museum. For a moment, then, a woman 'makes history'. But the whole number is riddled with contradictions, which revolve round the very problem of having an image of a woman acting historically.

Table 5.3

Self-willed	Mindless
Miller as star (R)	Miller's image ('magnificent animal') (R)
Miller character – decision-maker in narrative (R)	Number set in anthropology museum – associations with primitivism (R)
Tap as self-expressive form (NR)	Tap as mindless repetitions (NR)
Improvisatory routine (R/NR)	

31

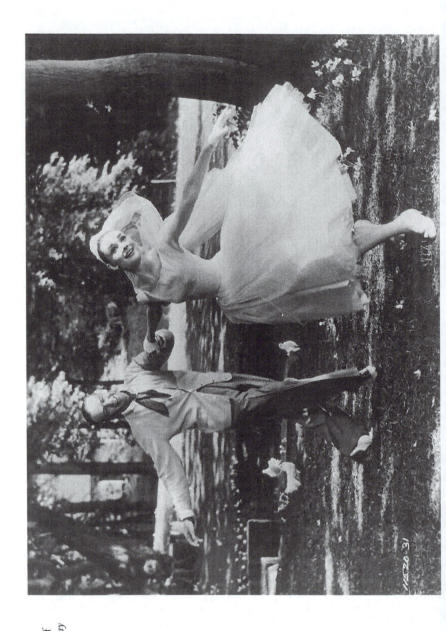

Figure 5.2
The *mise-en-scène* of transparency: *Funny Face*

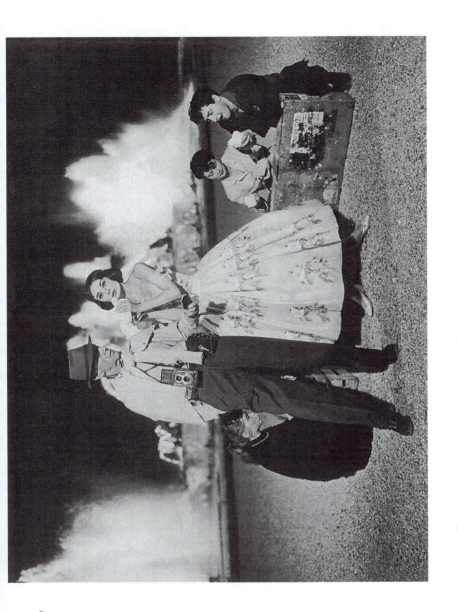

Figure 5.3
Constructing
transparency: *Funny
Face*

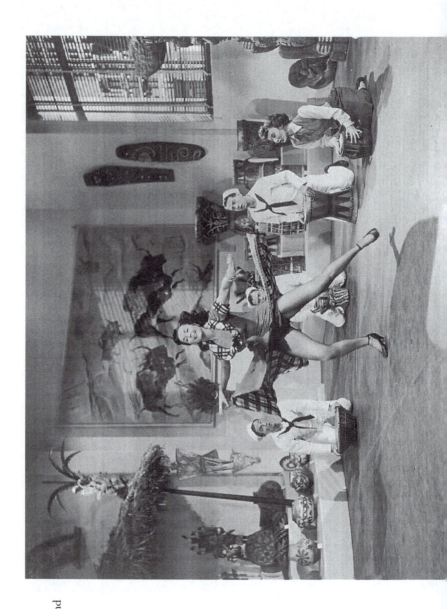

Figure 5.4
Energy from
Ann Miller and
primitivism:
On the Town

If we take the number and her part in it to pieces (Table 5.3), we can see that it plays on an opposition between self-willed and mindless modes of being; and this play is between representational (R) and non-representational (NR) at all aesthetic levels.

The idea of a historical utopianism in narrativity derives from the work of Ernest Bloch. According to Frederic Jameson, Bloch

> has essentially two different languages or terminological systems at his disposition to describe the formal nature of Utopian fulfilment: the movement of the world in time towards the future's ultimate moment, and the more spatial notion of that adequation of object to subject which must characterise that moment's content ... [These] correspond to dramatic and lyrical modes of the presentation of not-yet-being.
>
> (1971: 146)

Musicals (and Variety) represent an extra ordinary mix of these two modes – the historicity of narrative and the lyricism of numbers. They have not often taken advantage of it, but the point is that they could, and that this possibility is always latent in them. They are a form we still need to look at if films are, in Brecht's words on the theatre, to 'organize the enjoyment of changing reality'.

Movie 24, 1977

References

Enzensberger, Hans Magnus (1972) 'Constituents of a theory of the media', in Denis McQuail (ed.) *Sociology of Mass Communications*, Harmondsworth: Penguin, 99–116.
Jameson, Fredric (1971) *Marxism and Form*, Princeton, NJ: Princeton University Press.
Kateb, George (1972) *Utopia and its Enemies*, New York: Schocken.
Langer, Susanne K. (1953) *Feeling and Form*, London: Routledge & Kegan Paul.
Trilling, Lionel (1972) *Sincerity and Authenticity*, London: Oxford University Press.

Further reading

Altman, Rick (ed.) (1981) *Genre: The Musical*, London: Routledge & Kegan Paul.
Altman, Rick (1987) *The American Film Musical*, Bloomington IN: Indiana University Press.
Feuer, Jane (1982) *The Hollywood Musical*, London: Macmillan.
Flinn, Caryl (1992) *Strains of Utopia*, Princeton, NJ: Princeton University Press.
Gaines, Jane and Herzog, Charlotte (eds) (1990) *Fabrications: Costume and the Female Body*, London and New York: Routledge.
Geraghty, Christine (1991) *Women and Soap Opera*, Cambridge: Polity Press.
Lovell, Terry (1980) *Pictures of Reality*, London: British Film Institute.
Modleski, Tania (1982) *Loving with a Vengeance*, New York: Methuen.
Williams, Linda (1990) *Hard Core: the Frenzy of the Visible*, Berkeley, CA: University of California Press.

6

THE COLOUR OF
ENTERTAINMENT

In the middle of *That's Entertainment! III*, the last of MGM's compilation of highlights from its musicals, Lena Horne remarks that it was not alway so very jolly working on these paeans to happiness. She says it mildly, iron ically, in a tone of probable conciliation, but it comes over like a flash o lightning on a sunny summer's day.

It's not that she's complaining about the work, though she, or any of th other hosts in the film, might well do. The *That's Entertainment!* series ha never been inclined to dwell on it, but everyone has always known that ther was as much grind as merriment in making these movies. If common sens were not enough to tell us that you don't get all those elements – music dance, costume, decor, camerawork – into such perfect condition and s perfectly coordinated without labouring at it, there have been plenty of histo ries and memoirs to remind us. The time, the heat, the discomfort, to sa nothing of the unpleasantness of some of the key personnel – Louis B. Mayer' manipulative cruelty, Arthur Freed's womanizing and fag-baiting – are wel documented. Making that jolly tale of the road to happiness, *The Wizard o Oz*, sounds like it was misery from end to end.

Nor is Horne saying anything she hasn't said before. In her biographies in interviews, most memorably in her stage show *Lena Horne: the Lady an Her Music*, Horne has recounted the racism she encountered at MGM (an throughout her career): the attempts to persuade her to pretend she wasn' black, the racially coded criticisms of her style (for instance, that she mad her mouth too big when she sang), the chronic inability to use her excep in self-contained numbers dropped into the films and easily cut out fo Southern exhibition, the scandal of her marrying a white man. The very fac that someone as magnetic and beautiful as her stopped working for MGN in 1950, long before the musical's fortunes started to decline, has alway itself been eloquent testimony to her treatment there. And, inadvertently MGM let us glimpse all this in the first *That's Entertainment!* film, in sequence showing the MGM stars gathered together at an anniversary dinner The camera tracks along and shows us the stars being themselves: Jud Garland bubbling, Clark Gable grinning, Greer Garson in period costume

Katharine Hepburn talking, talking – and Lena, silent, staring into middle distance, looking frankly pissed off. Even then, for those who cared to read it, her body language conveyed what her words make explicit in *That's Entertainment! III*.

So it's no sense of revelation that makes Horne's contribution to *TE3* so startling. It is rather the context of it. All the other hosts – in this and the other films in the series (including *That's Dancing!* as well as *TE* and *TE2*) – have assured us that at MGM life was nothing but fun, respect and fulfilling hard work. We don't believe it, but the idea that it was is itself part of the entertainment on offer. As Jane Feuer discusses in her book, *The Hollywood Musical* (1982), the show-within-a-show format of so many musicals both shows the labour and skill involved in putting on an entertainment and passes it all off as improvisation, spontaneity, community, fellowship and having a good time. So it is with the *That's Entertainment!* movies, and it comes as a shock to have someone even suggest anything to the contrary.

What makes Horne's segment more startling still is what comes before and after it. Before, we have a number called 'Pass That Peace Pipe' from *Good News*, brilliantly performed by the forgotten Joan McCracken and a host of people pretending to be college boys and girls. After it, we have Judy Garland, her voice strained and sporting a fright wig, in 'I'm an Indian Too', one of the numbers she shot for *Annie Get Your Gun* before she left it. Presented in *TE3* without comment, both numbers are based on the premises that it's fine for whites to do cod versions of Native American dance movements and that there is something intrinsically hilarious about Native American names – so 'Pass That Peace Pipe' has merry tongue twisters such as 'just like the Choctaws, Chickasaws, Chattanooga Chippewas do', while 'I'm an Indian Too' has the refrain, 'A Sioux-oo-oo, a Sioux-oo-oo'. So here we have Lena Horne raising the film's racial consciousness and the film carrying on as if she has said not a thing.

Horne's contribution puts onto the agenda the whole question of race and musicals of the MGM variety (which were not exclusively made by MGM – *Cover Girl*, *Funny Face* or *Hello Dolly!* are all 'MGM musicals', even though they were made by Columbia, Paramount and Fox respectively). She prompts us to look past the opulence and dynamism of the numbers assembled by the film to consider the racial character of the entertainment promoted by the musical genre.

This is not just a question of the way the non-white peoples of the United States are represented, though heaven knows there are plenty of sins of omission and commission on this front. The former are perhaps the more staggering. Let us stick here just with African-Americans, the fount of US popular music, itself one of the greatest glories of twentieth-century culture. Let us also grant that there is too much pain, bitterness and defiance in people like Billie Holiday or Paul Robeson for them to be easily accommodated with the musical's gospel of gaiety. But think what feelgood black

Figure 6.1 Lena Horne, 1943

talent there was available that was either not used or squandered: Nat King Cole, Billy Eckstein, Ella Fitzgerald, Eartha Kitt, Sarah Vaughan, for starters, and dancers like Honi Coles or Katherine Dunham, whose names are perhaps less familiar precisely because they were so little recorded on film. Even when people like Louis Armstrong, Pearl Bailey, Cab Calloway, the Nicholas Brothers, Bill Robinson, Hazel Scott, Ethel Waters or, of course, Lena Horne

38

were used, it was nearly always in one kind of ghetto or another: the all-black musical, the number that can be dropped without doing violence to either the story or the editing (such as Horne's intense 'Where or When' in *Words and Music*) or, in the case of the sublime Bill Robinson, kiddie's corner, squiring Shirley Temple. All of these do at least preserve such performances on film and, as Donald Bogle argues in his *Toms, Coons, Mulattoes, Mammies and Bucks* (1973), what these performers achieve in these moments far outstrips the limitations of the space and role allotted them. There is generally something to be salvaged from even the most unpromising examples: not only are Robinson's performances with Temple such superb examples of his swinging, up-on-the-toes style, they also provide one of the few images we have of rapport between an adult male and a female child that is neither smarmy nor (usually simultaneously) sinister. Yet what we know of him elsewhere make us realize how severely Hollywood restricted his range and thus what magic it passed up, again.

Black performers in MGM-style musicals nearly always play characters who are nothing but entertainers (the exceptions are the few all-black musicals). They may be – often are – slaves, servants, waiters, prostitutes, but all they ever do in those roles is entertain. This is how it has been in the movies for a long time: when the white Southerners in *The Birth of a Nation* show their white Northern friends round the plantation, what they show them are blacks dancing. Usually, blacks in musicals explicitly play professional entertainers, typically club acts seen by the white characters on a night out. Musicals are of course very often about characters who are entertainers, but when they're white, they usually also have lives, especially love lives but also careers, vexatious relatives, personal problems of one kind or another. No such wider life is given the black characters (if one can really call them characters), which deprives their appearances of the emotional resonances that the surrounding story and characterization give to numbers in musicals.

Blackness is contained in the musical, ghettoized, stereotyped, trapped in the category of 'only entertainment'. Yet containment is the antithesis of the entertainment that the musical offers. Bursting from the confines of life by singing your heart out and dancing when you feel like it, this is the joy of the musical. It is in whites' privilege to be able to do this, and what it tells us about the white dream of being in the world, that the musical most disturbingly constructs a vision of race.

It's to do with a relation to both physical space and also to the cultural spaces of other peoples. This is a given of the fundamental performance elements of the musical, dance and song. Dancing is by definition about bodies in space, about how bodies relate to other bodies, how they move through space, how they make use of or submit to the environment around them. Less obviously, singing too is about space; singing carries into space in a different way from speech and different kinds of singing, from crooning to belting, impose themselves differently on the world around the singer.

Fred Astaire's light voice and deft delivery create an intimacy that envelopes just him and his partner – no-one notices when he croons 'Cheek to Cheek' to Ginger Rogers on a crowded dance floor in *Top Hat*, before gliding her away to a secluded area. By contrast, at the end of "'S Wonderful' in *An American in Paris*, Gene Kelly and Georges Guetary move further and further away from each other down a Parisian street, yelling alternately to each other the exultation of being in love:

'S wonderful!	'S wonderful!
'S exceptional!	'S why I fell!
C'est magnifique!	'S what I seek!
C'élégant!	'S what I want!
C'est quelque chose!	From head to toes!
'S wonderful!	'S marvellous!
That she should care for me!	

They dominate the street and passers-by look fondly on at, no doubt, *les folies de l'amour*.

Musicals typically show us space entirely occupied by white people, dancing wherever they want, singing as loudly or intimately as they need. This is often, as it is with black performers, contained within the confines of the space of entertainment, the theatre or cabaret stage. Even then this was an extraordinarily elastic space, especially in the hands of a Busby Berkeley in the Warner Brothers musicals of the 1930s. However, it was one of the distinctions of the MGM tradition to break away from exclusive show-within-a-show presentation, to give us singing in the rain and dancing in the street. This is where it began to be difficult to make better use of black performers.

One of the loveliest numbers in all of the MGM musicals is 'Main Street' in *On the Town*. It is gloriously simple: the setting is a bare rehearsal studio, the performers wear their characters' everyday clothes, the melody is relaxed, the words plain and the dance steps seem little more than choreographed strolling, skipping and child's play. In short, 'Main Street' says 'anyone can do this and be so happy'. In the song, Gene Kelly invites Vera-Ellen to imagine they are back in his small town, Meadowville, in middle America, walking down the main street together. The name of the town and street are archetypes of ordinariness. As they dance, in their imagination they rejoice in the warmth and freedom of American ordinariness. But down how many main streets in how many small US towns can we imagine a black couple strolling with such unwary joy? This is not to demand that the musical be realistic, but rather to suggest how even the utopian imagination has its boundaries of plausibility. 'Main Street' works because it feels psychically right to imagine whites – but only whites – so at ease in the heartland of the United States.

This feeling is intensified in numbers which start from a transition from a more confined to a more open space. It's not always easy to get the impact of this from the *That's Entertainment!* films, which generally only give us the numbers (usually incomplete), not the situations from which the numbers arise. *TE3* includes, for instance, 'The Heather on the Hill' from *Brigadoon* and we do have the thrill of Cyd Charisse and Gene Kelly running up the hill and dancing along its brow, but the song itself (which precedes the dance) is cut as well as the surrounding narrative context. In their run and dance, we feel something of the romanticism of sublime high places and picturesque landscapes, but we miss the awareness developed in the story of the restrictions on heterosexual relations and the rather more arcane limitations on all relationships in the doomed village of Brigadoon. The feeling of fresh air and open spaces of 'The Heather on the Hill', the emphasis on uplift in the dancing, all these have their meaning in the way they embody the characters' excitement at transcending the constraints on their lives. It is the equivalents of these that make so many great numbers soar: Gene Kelly, Rita Hayworth and Phil Silvers striding out of their favourite bar into the street in *Cover Girl* to 'Make Way for Tomorrow!'; the coda to 'My Favourite Things' in *The Sound of Music*, cutting from Julie Andrews sitting in her bedroom wondering what to do with these miserable kids to a montage of her leading them on a free-wheeling gambol round Salzburg, winding up on a mountain top ready for the next number, 'Do Re Mi'; the bullied underlings who decide to 'Put on [their] Sunday Clothes', strut out of the house, down the street and off to New York in *Hello Dolly!* Black people doing the same thing would in the white imagination seem like a terrifying attempt to take over.

Yet what whites do to their environment in these numbers is precisely to take it over. In all the examples I've given so far, the space they've taken over is already a white space, one that society entitles them to, but the underlying structure of feeling is of the right to expand out into space, whoever it belongs to. Something of this is evident in another scintillating number from *On the Town*, 'Prehistoric Man', which starts off with Ann Miller telling Jules Munshin in the New York Museum of Natural History that she fancies him far more than the average modern male because he looks like a cave man. Once the dancing gets under way, Miller leads the group (Munshin, Betty Garrett, Gene Kelly and Frank Sinatra) in an unabashed, high-energy exploration of the museum. They use what is to hand to express their libidinal enthusiasm and the natural history to hand turns out to be the pickings of 'primitive' culture. So there are tom-toms, Arabic instruments, bear skins, wigwams and so on, all grist to white joy. The number – and precisely in its intoxicating exuberance – is the very model of the colonial structure of feeling: expansion into space, control over what's in that space, incorporation of what's there into white agendas. This movement of expansion and incorporation is at the heart of the musical's construction of race.

'Prehistoric Man' romps through the spoils of a space that has already been expanded into: the museum is a repository of white exploration and colonialism. The musical has often been prepared to go further, actually to enter that space (as long as it could recreate it in the studio, of course). The early MGM musicals based on operettas were sometimes explicitly about colonialism: *Naughty Marietta, The Desert Song, Rose Marie, The Firefly.* In other musicals, the non-white world is oddly free of non-white people: there are no blacks on the Caribbean island of *The Pirate*, for instance, no Native Americans in *Oklahoma!* Even a race-sensitive musical like *South Pacific* celebrates the lustiness of white GIs (and one or two black ones) in 'There is Nothing Like a Dame', performed all over a Polynesian beach devoid of Polynesians, save the old woman, Bloody Mary, who caters to their wants (drugs, booze, women).

One of the out-takes featured in *TE3* is 'The March of the Doagies' from *The Harvey Girls,* a Judy Garland musical set in the West. The number shows townsfolk striding out into the surrounding country in celebration mood. With the relentless onward surge of its massed movements and firm editing and its torchlight *mise-en-scène*, it looks like nothing so much as a gathering of the Klans. This is taking possession of the land with a vengeance. No wonder it was dropped. It makes explicit what is masked in an earlier number in the film, 'On the Atcheson, Topeka and the Santa Fe', which shows the film's heroines arriving on the eponymous train at the township that is to be their new home. The number – justly prized by *aficionados* of the genre – has a complex interplay of both featured singers and choreographed movement and camerawork; it has a great, catchy tune, given rousing but also ruminative and humorous variations; and it is a superb example of a number that expands outwards, as people step down from their long train journey and out into the new township, with the space for song and dance, for release and exhilaration, ever widening as the number proceeds, the interplay of elements evoking an instant (as well as literal) harmony, culminating in a splendid unison dance alongside the train as it pulls out. It has all the brio and spontaneity lacking from 'The March of the Doagies' – yet it too is about possession of the land: the song celebrates one of the main instruments by which this was achieved, the railway, while the number shows white folks in the joyous occupancy of the world.

Whites in musicals have this rapturous relationship with their environment. This may be confined to the utopian moments of the numbers, but then they are the reason we go to see musicals. The potentially colonialist nature of this is suggested not only by the way whites stride down streets as if they own them (which in a certain sense they usually do) and burst all over other locales (which they don't), but also in the way the cultures of the colonized, as perceived by whites, are incorporated into the musical and terpsichorean fabric of the numbers. This is evident in 'Prehistoric Man', not just in the ethnographic objects picked out and played with by the dancers but also in the way they adapt their movements by adopting gestures, shapes and even sounds from 'ethnic' dance: a bit of bottom wiggling for Ann Miller when she gets hold of some Arab instruments, some bent over high stepping and Red Indian hollering for Betty Garrett when she puts on a Native American head-dress, and stomps and 'ugh' sounds when all five of them get hold of some African tom-toms.

The musical's propensity to do this sort of thing is sent up in the brilliant 'Stereophonic Sound' number in *Silk Stockings*, in which Fred Astaire and delicious Janis Paige mock the commercial imperatives of the day (more spectacle, hang the plot). At one point they sing of how it's not enough to have dancing any more, you have to have 'Russian ballet, or Chinese ballet, or Bali ballet, or any ballet', and with each one they take up, with extraordinary precision and speed, a pose that sums up the national style in question. Numbers that have no overall non-US cultural reference do this all the time, slip into a bit of 'African' here, a bit of 'Irish' there, and so on. We are all familiar with the repertoire: syncopated stomping, with head and shoulders bent forward, is 'Red Indian'; side-ways movements of the head, with hands touching above it, is 'Indian' (as in India); fast stamping heels and bent arms circling round the body is 'Spanish'; and anything that flaunts hips, groin and arse is 'black'. Singing, and especially orchestrations, can do the same sort of thing. The exactness and rapidity with which it is done are generally breathtaking.

You might see this as eclectic, as a generous recognition of the music and dance riches of other cultures. It could even sound like a postmodern hybridity *avant la lettre*. There is undoubtedly a felt need to refresh and enliven white music and dance, indeed, white life and spirits, with the vitality, sensuality and sheer difference of other cultures. Yet all of the latter are subsumed into white needs, white goals, white displays. This is, after all, not dancing with the Other, but incorporating it, literally taking the Other into one's own body.

There is even an implication that whites are better at black (and other) music and dance than blacks themselves. The greatest Southern black routine in musicals may well be shiningly pink Ann Miller's 'Shakin' the Blues Away' in *Easter Parade*, a *tour de force* of tapping and shimmying. While the black roots of taps may have been forgotten or never known to white audiences by the time this first appeared (1948), shimmies were the 'black' movement *par excellence* in the white imagination. And, were this not enough, the song, though it never mentions skin colour, is all about what 'they' do 'down South', and it sure as anything can't mean that this kind of cavorting is what white Southern ladies and gentlemen get up to.

If Ann Miller does the greatest Southern black routine, then the greatest exponent of the black art of tap dance is Fred Astaire (and I'm Cyd Charisse). His case is interesting. In *Swing Time*, he blacks up to pay tribute to his sources, and specifically to Bill Robinson, in the 'Bojangles of Harlem' number. Generously meant, no doubt, but the use of blackface cannot help but be disturbing (even if it is quite far from the grotesqueries of minstrelsy), and wouldn't it have been better if Astaire had used his influence to get Robinson himself on screen? Gerald Mast, in *Can't Help Singing* (1987) commends the several numbers in which Astaire dances with black men (not women, presumably because this would raise the question of sexuality): 'Slap that Bass' in *Shall We Dance?*, a number with black and white prisoners in *You'll Never Get Rich* and, perhaps most famously, 'Shine on Your Shoes' in *The Band Wagon*. The latter takes place in an amusement arcade on 42nd Street; the number starts off from the rhythm of the shoe shine 'boy', LeRoy Daniels, doing his job and leads into a *pas de deux* for him and Astaire. It is hardly an equal routine, however. Occasionally both men occupy the screen equally and do the same or equivalent movements, but for most of the time Daniels is choreographically subservient to Astaire. Daniels's happy-go-lucky shoe shining may give Astaire the inspiration to cheer up in this miserable amusement arcade (which symbolizes for him the decline of Broadway entertainment), dancing with a black dancer may signal recognition of the sources (and masters) of this tradition, but Daniels is really only there to provide a sunny rhythmic point of departure for Astaire's brilliance and his character's feelings of release.

Most numbers do not even go so far as Astaire's in acknowledging black and other ethnic sources. The lively quote, as in 'Prehistoric Man' or 'Stereophonic Sound', is one thing. Ready mastery of exotic dances, especially Latin American ones, is OK too. But the degree to which black and Hispanic music and dance are the foundations of US popular music cannot be acknowledged – it is incorporated so far in MGM musicals as to disappear from view.

That's Entertainment! III ends with 'That's Entertainment!' from *The Band Wagon*. It's a list song, laying out all the things that can be called 'entertainment', deliberately including Sophocles and Shakespeare alongside melodrama, comedy, 'the lights on the lady in tights' and 'the clown with his pants falling down'. It takes place on a theatre stage, with odds and ends of scenery on it. In the course of the number, the performers (Fred Astaire, Jack Buchanan, Cyd Charisse, Nanette Fabray and Oscar Levant) move from standing close together to moving over the whole area of the stage, using flats, hoists and props in a celebration of entertainment's wit, energy and spontaneity. Yet in all the song, there is not one mention of anything that could be called black, even though the music and dance called upon could not have existed without recourse to black (and other) cultural forms.

I've always rather balked at the final words of 'That's Entertainment!':

> The gag may be waving a flag
> That began with a Mr Cohan
> Hip hooray, the American way

44

The world is a stage
The stage is a world
Of entertainment!

– but I've always assumed this was excessive European sensitivity on my part. Now though I can't help reflecting upon the colour of entertainment in America itself and the way this has been processed so consummately by the MGM musical.

Sight and Sound 5 (11) (NS), 1995

References

Bogle, Donald (1973) *Toms, Coons, Mulattoes, Mammies and Bucks*, New York: Viking.
Feuer, Jane (1982) *The Hollywood Musical*, London: British Film Institute/Macmillan.
Mast, Gerald (1987) *Can't Help Singing: The American Musical on Stage and Screen*, Woodstock, NY: Overlook Press.

Further reading

Bogle, Donald (1980) *Brown Sugar: Eighty Years of America's Black Female Superstars*, New York: Da Capo.
Dyer, Richard (1998) 'The space of happiness in the musical', *Aura* 4 (1), 31–45.
McKinnon, Kenneth (2000) '"I keep wishing I were somewhere else": space and fantasies of freedom in the Hollywood musical', in Marshall, Bill and Stilwel, Robynn (eds) *Musicals*, Exeter: Intellect Books, 40–46.
Naremore, James 'Uptown folk: blackness and entertainment in *Cabin in the Sky*', and Knee, Adam 'Doubling, music, and race in *Cabin in the Sky*', in Gabbard, Krin (ed.) *Representing Jazz*, Durham, NC: Duke University Press, 169–92, 193–204.
Roberts, Shari (1993) Seeing Stars: Feminine Spectacle, Female Spectators and World War II, PhD thesis, University of Chicago.

7

THE SOUND OF MUSIC

This is an attempt at a cultural reading of *The Sound of Music*. It is ideological in two senses. First, it is neither science nor simple subjectivism. It does not produce unquestionable, definitive knowledge or Truth (as is claimed — wrongly — for the natural sciences, and religion), but nor is it just what I happen to think. Rather it applies, openly and recognizably, an ideological position to the reading of the film (whilst not ignoring the question of evidence). This position places the reading within a developed, available intellectual and political debate — something fundamentally different from both 'value-free' science and the elaboration of personal taste or morality. Second, it is concerned with the way the ideology of the dominant groups in our society (above all, the bourgeoisie and men) operates in and on the film.

My argument is that in the case of *The Sound of Music*, the film sets up human (but also specifically female) problems, and solutions to them, that by implication run counter to the interests, and hence ideology, of the dominant groups. The film attempts to recoup this through various narrative and musical procedures (not through the conscious or conspiratorial intervention of the ruling groups, but because it is always more comfortable to fit in with dominant ideology — entertainment always seeks a point of comfort, whatever its point of departure). It seems likely that this pattern is very typical of Hollywood cinema, and perhaps especially of its supremely successful films.

Following the classic pattern of the musical, *The Sound of Music* is a movement between the narrative (in which problems, tensions and contradictions are set up) and the numbers (in which they are resolved or evaded). The narrative works chiefly, but not exclusively, through its representational, verisimilitudinous elements — the plot situations, the character types, the star images and so on. These are the elements people 'identify' with, and it is reasonable to hypothesize that the success of *The Sound of Music* is partly due to their managing to embody, dirndls notwithstanding, central problems and tensions in the lives of its predominantly female audience. In the case of the numbers, we have to pay more attention to the non-representational, sensuous-formal elements: music, movement, colour, texture and so

46

on. These are not 'pure' or 'mere' forms, but rather embodiments of feeling. I follow here Susanne Langer's analysis of the artistic sign, whose meaning (or 'import' in her terminology) comes from the resemblance of the sign's shape and structure to the shape and structure of human feeling. Analysing the sensuous level of artistic signification means grasping the links between the formal, culturally developed rules of an artistic tradition (in this case, romantic popular music, Hollywood style, show business traditions) and a sensibility which is crucially, but probably not wholly, determined by a specific culture. The tone and form of the numbers indicate, to use Raymond Williams's term, a culture's 'structure of feeling'. Both narrative and numbers, it should be stressed, are fields in which the dominant ideology may – and will always try to – operate, although the numbers especially tend to present themselves as pure realms of feeling, beyond ideology or even beyond culture.

What happens

For anyone who has not seen the film recently (or at all), here is an outline of what happens in it, noting particularly where the numbers enter the narrative.

Section 1

Maria (Julie Andrews) sings 'The Sound of Music' on a hilltop. Peal of (we later learn) abbey bells sends her rushing off downhill. Credits sequence, with overture, including information that film is set in Salzburg 'in the last golden days of the 'thirties'. – Sung prayers in abbey ('*Dixit Dominus*', 'Allelujah'); several sisters complain ('Maria') to Mother Abbess (Peggy Wood) about novice Maria, who is late for prayers, bad-mannered and tactless; they are momentarily interrupted by Maria returning in haste from hills. – Mother Abbess advises Maria that spell in outside world might help her make up mind whether she really feels called to be nun; Maria sent to be governess to seven children of Captain von Trapp; leaving abbey Maria is nervous, but builds up courage by singing 'Confidence'. – Maria much impressed by beauty of von Trapp mansion, less impressed with Captain (Christopher Plummer) who orders home with severity, rules and regulations. – After dinner, eldest daughter Liesl (Charmian Carr) sneaks out of house to meet local delivery boy Rolf (Dan Truhitte) in grounds; 'You Are Sixteen'; they dance in summer-house as thunderstorm begins. – Liesl climbs back into house through Maria's bedroom window; they are joined by other children, frightened by thunder; Maria cheers them with 'My Favourite Things'; interrupted by Captain, appalled at singing; he also announces departure for Vienna next day. – Alone in room, Maria sings 'My Favourite Things' to self, leading to montage of Maria and children visiting Salzburg and playing; on hilltop, Maria gives them singing lesson, 'Do Re Mi'. – Captain returns with Baroness (Eleanor Parker) and Max (Richard Haydn), an impresario looking for folk acts for Salzburg festival; Captain shocked at appearance and liveliness of children, but Baroness charmed when they sing 'The Sound of Music' to her. – Maria and children put on puppet show for Captain and guests: 'The Lonely Goatherd'.

Section 2

After show, Liesl persuades Captain to sing; chooses 'Edelweiss'; Baroness silently observes Maria's attractiveness. – To please Baroness, Captain throws lavish ball; children and Maria watch from verandah; Maria teaches oldest boy Friedrich (Nicholas Hammond) the Ländler, an Austrian dance; half-way through Captain takes Friedrich's place, as Baroness watches; children say good-night in song, 'So Long, Farewell'; Baroness tells Maria Captain has fallen for her; anxious, Maria slips out of house. – Intermission. – Maria returns to abbey, where Mother Abbess tells her that she must not run away from problems but face them, 'Climb Every Mountain'. – Maria returns to von Trapp household in time to join in with children singing, rather lugubriously, 'My Favourite Things'. – Marriage of Baroness and Captain announced, but Baroness realizes where Captain's feelings really are, and regretfully sends him out into grounds where Maria is wandering; in summerhouse they express love, 'Something Good'. – Spectacular wedding scene. 'Maria' integrated with organ processional hymn.

Section 3

Returning from honeymoon, Captain and Maria find Max has entered children in festival; Captain forbids it, but when realizes life and family threatened by Nazis, consents to appearing with children and Maria in attempt to foil Nazis. – Under cover of festival, where they're awarded first prize, they escape hiding for moment in abbey, over mountains to Switzerland ('Climb Every Mountain' over).

Section 1

The first part of *The Sound of Music*, up to and including 'The Lonely Goatherd', is structured around an opposition, which is lived out as a conflict of feeling by the heroine, Maria. This opposition is between two realms of existence – the first, totalitarian, represented by the abbey and then by the von Trapp household; the second, free, spontaneous and experiential embodied in the experience of music.

The two opening numbers of the film, 'The Sound of Music' and the abbey sequence (sung prayers, 'Maria') express the opposition clearly. The first sum up from the word go what music means for the heroine and the film. Music is identified with nature, nature as conceived by the Romantics. The camera takes us down from the cold, bare regions of the mountain-tops to the lush, green world of the hills. This is a natural world, but one into which humanity can fit harmoniously. It is the fulfilment of the promise of the background music, affirming that the hills are indeed not just accompanied by music but alive with it. The lyrics of the song pick on close detail, where a natural sound translates to a musical or human one, and where the dynamics of this sound correspond to the dynamics of human feeling:

> My HEART wants to *beat like* the wings of a *bird* that flies from
>   the lake to the trees,
> To SIGH *like* a chime from a *bell* that flies from the church on a
>   *breeze*,
> To LAUGH *like* a *brook* as it leaps and falls over stones on its way,
> To *sing* through the night *like a lark* that is learning to PRAY.

The last line draws attention to a further affirmation of the song, that the music of nature is a form of religious experience, but not so much Christian as direct contact with the essential and the everlasting:

> The hills fill my heart with the sound of music,
> With songs they have heard *for a thousand years* . . .
> My heart will be *blessed* with the sound of music
> And I'll sing once more.

The import of this song – the innate musicality of nature, Maria's identification with it, its ability to inspire her to song – is underlined by cutting from Maria on the hilltop to her wandering among trees, along a brook, or picked out against the sky in the final affirmation (the last two lines quoted above).

This 'free' editing (following the logic of the song, not geography) combines with the sweeping camerawork, the full-bodied singing and the wide open spaces to define music as spontaneity, freedom, the untrammelled outpouring of pure feeling. In this, *The Sound of Music* is drawing on conceptions of music widespread in our culture. It is very commonly believed that music is a pure realm of feeling, beyond ideology. Here ideology is identified with politics, business, advertising, the rat race – realms of manipulation, alienation, unfreedom. This definition of music in a sense precludes any understanding of a positive, participatory, non-alienative ideology by pointing to an absolute, nature-music, that is beyond any imaginable culture or society. It is a measure of the sense of manipulation and alienation among people in this society that, quite by accident no doubt, in one of its most popular films the ideal identified as the non-ideological is so insistently evoked.

By contrast with this sequence, the musical world of the abbey is ordered, ritual, formal. After the sweeping camera and free editing of 'The Sound of Music', the *'Dixit Dominus'* is static, measured. Each shot is carefully composed, with balanced lighting, still camera. A sequence of close-ups of nuns at prayer emphasizes the conventionality of this world – there are either the young, fresh, innocent faces of novices, clean and scrubbed and healthy, or the older, lined, wise yet still innocent faces of the higher orders. We see no one middle-aged or ugly. Again, during the song 'Maria', the camera remains static, and formal composition of groups of nuns standing in the courtyard is used throughout. The bounce of the tune is not reproduced by the staging, which remains rigid and formal. Before the last line of the song, Maria bursts into the abbey, hair tousled, not looking where she is going. The nuns look at her, then sing slowly, in 'reverent' harmony: 'How do you hold a moonbeam in your hand?' This catches exactly how Maria fits into their world – she cannot be pinned down, she shatters the style of abbey life and yet she is magical too, charming and indefinable. They feel the pull of 'music', just as she does.

Although there is music in the abbey, it represents an approach to life quite different from that shown in the opening sequence, and this approach is elaborated by what we learn of the abbey and Maria's inability to fit into its highly structured life. The rules, written and unwritten, of abbey life cramp Maria's style, stifle her musicality, seem to cut out the freedom that music asserts. She is unable to remember prayer times, to keep her mouth shut and stop arguing, and for much of the time this is played for laughs, as when Maria says of the sister who makes her kiss the floor after an argument: 'Now I kiss the floor when I see her coming to save time!' But Maria's attitude towards the abbey is ambivalent – vexing as life is there, she feels greatly drawn to it, not only because of the goodness of the nuns but because she was drawn to the abbey during her girlhood reveries on the mountains. Despite all its restrictions, there is something in the abbey that corresponds to what Maria finds in the hills. She too feels the pull of 'order'.

In the von Trapp household, the opposition is more stark – music and silence. Captain von Trapp has banned music, and most speech, from the house. He has organized the lives of the children and servants so rigidly that they answer to the call of a whistle and follow a strict pattern of daily life. The 'natural' bubbling spontaneity of the children has been systematically suppressed. It is against this totalitarian regime (Figure 7.1), iconographically summed up in the cold thin lips, acid blue eyes and militarily precise dress of Christopher Plummer's Captain von Trapp, that Maria must assert, with renewed force, her musicality.

At this stage in the film, Maria is attempting to make the world a world of music. This is expressed in the transition song from the abbey to the von Trapp household, 'Confidence'. The lyrics of the song express Maria's confidence in herself and in the world, her determination to show herself and the world what she can do. It is sung in a forceful manner, with a complete sureness of pitch and a confident breaking of the musical line (e.g. consider the way Julie Andrews turns the middle section almost into an harangue: 'Strength doesn't lie in numbers! Strength doesn't lie in wealth! Strength lies in hours of peaceful slumbers, when you wake up, get up! it's healthy!') Her movements are a determined stride forward and, towards the end, a leaping movement, clicking the heels together. In the length of the song Maria moves from the abbey to the von Trapp home – as in the journey number, 'Don't Rain on my Parade', in *Funny Girl*, the song remains intact while the stages of the journey are seen only briefly, edited together. Not only does the song remain intact, but whenever we see the heroine, no matter what stage of the journey she has reached, she is still singing the song and is at the right moment in the song. The action is telescoped to fit the song, the logic of the real world gives way to the logic of the song, of music. And as in *Funny Girl*, nothing could be more appropriate, for by it we see the world come under the control and determination of the heroine, whose very essence is music. In the rest of the first part of the film, which is incidentally the richest in musical numbers, the concepts lying behind the notion of 'music' are elaborated. Each number deepens the picture.

'My Favourite Things' is the occasion for the demonstration of music's power to banish the fears of the real world. The children have run to Maria's room, terrified by the thunderstorm. To cheer them up, she asks them to think of nice things like kittens, rainbows, snow, and out of the list develops the song. But it is essentially the *music* that cheers, not thinking of the nice things, for when, later in the film (after Maria has temporarily left the von Trapps), the children attempt to reprise the song, the result is lugubrious, dispirited. It is only when Maria returns during the attempted reprise, and in her singing recovers the song's bounce, that it is effective. This is because 'My Favourite Things', despite its lyrics, expresses in the way it is presented more the essential spontaneity and warm community of music than the comfort of nice thoughts. As Maria lists the nice things, the inherent rhythm of the natural speech is picked up pizzicato on the strings, which thus lifts the list into the lilt of the song. The song develops 'spontaneously' from the natural rhythms of speech; music follows 'naturally' as the list calls forth joyfulness. The editing of the song is remarkable, for the sureness of touch with which one shot follows another (in the fairly small space of Maria's bedroom) gives the sense of the whole number being filmed continuously – as on live television, the performers sing and romp straight through the number, whilst the director cuts from camera to camera. Except that if you look closely, you see that it cannot possibly have been done like that, since there would be cameras in shot and a quite alarming number of them at that. But through the editing (the editor is William Reynolds and the director Robert Wise, who began his career as an editor), the perfect illusion is given of a spontaneously generated sense of togetherness being 'captured' by the camera.

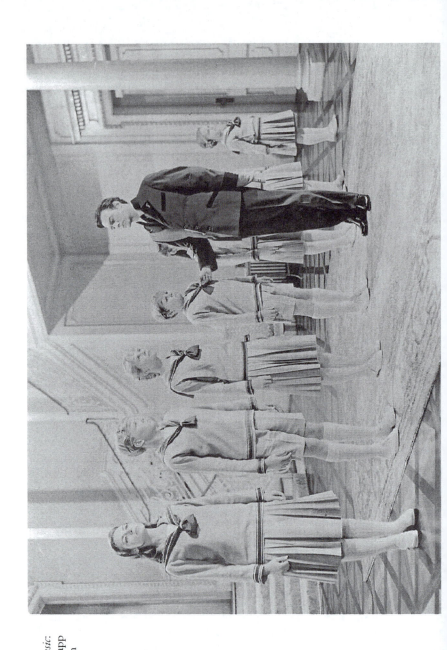

Figure 7.1
The Sound of Music:
Captain von Trapp
and the children

Figure 7.2
The Sound of Music:
Maria and the
children

'Do Re Mi' emphasizes first of all that it is singing itself which is fun. This is an extremely important point, for whilst the film certainly suggests varying ways in which music is important, it never allows it to be merely symbolic. Music does not 'stand for' other things, but is the locus of other values. It is crucial to assert the physical pleasure of music itself, the joy of singing in its own right. Hence the singing lesson concentrates on the notes and how to put them together, and not on what singing makes you feel or what you can express through it. Singing is *sui generis*. But, again, the staging presents a further dimension. It starts on a hilltop, much the same setting as for 'The Sound of Music', but as the number develops and the children pick up the notes and the melody, the song takes off into a sequence of shots in and around Salzburg (Figure 7.2), the children and Maria dancing along a river-bank, riding bicycles, imitating the poses of statues. Here again, this free editing, shaped by musical rather than real-world logic, conveys the extent to which music takes over the world – or feels as if it does to the singers. The rhythms of the editing convey the dynamics of the experience as it feels to the participants.

'The Lonely Goatherd' is performed as a puppet show by Maria and the children to please the Captain and the Baroness. The puppets act out a story which is just hinted at in the song's lyrics – a red-cheeked, dopey-looking boy is bashful with a pretty, long-eyelashed girl; her mother 'with a gleaming gloat' pushes her into the boy's arms, the prelude to their marriage and happiness. The story is re-enacted by a pair of goats (the female again having long eyelashes) and their story rounds off with two baby goats.

Much of 'The Lonely Goatherd' expresses again the sheer pleasure of making music. For much of the time the song is not saddled with a lyric at all, but simply consists of yodelling, the pure joy of musical utterance. This occurs, however, within a context which is of some interest: it is the context of a complete certainty about the nature of the world, or, to be more specific, the context of a firmly held common-sense view of sexual relationships. This view has two central points – the difference between the sexes and the manner by which marriage is achieved.

In 'The Lonely Goatherd', there is no problem about knowing what the difference between the sexes is (over and above the obvious physical differences). The images of the goatherd and the girl express in grotesque miniature a certainty which is expressed elsewhere in the film – for instance, when Maria pleads with von Trapp on behalf of his children: each one is presented as having a specific need for the Captain, based not on his or her individuality, but on their sex and the stage they have reached. Thus the eldest girl, being at that age and being a girl, needs freedom to have boyfriends without losing the assurance that her father still cares; the eldest boy, just at the turn of adolescence, needs to feel his father's support but – 'of course' – is too proud to show it; and so on, down to the youngest child, too little a person to want anything but 'just to love you'. People are transparent, sex and age determinant.

Equally certain in the antics of the puppets is the view that life is structured around female manipulation of the male, through prettiness in youth and domination in middle-age. To some extent both this and the view of sexual differences are borne out by subsidiary characters and scenes in the film – the children are not developed much as individuals; the Baroness is most adept at 'handling' von Trapp whilst Max Detweiler is weak and venial; there is irony in the scene between Rolf and Liesl, where he tells her to rely on him because he is 'older and wiser'. But, as we shall see, this certainty is not quite so firm in Maria and von Trapp as the film develops.

'The Sound of Music', 'My Favourite Things', 'Do Re Mi' and 'The Lonely Goatherd', taken together, represent the realm of freedom and joy, of music, as against the formality and restrictions of the abbey and the silence and rigidity of the von Trapp household. A further dimension to this opposition, not expressed directly in music, is that of class. Maria is of peasant origins, a fact that the film stresses. It gives a further validity to her spontaneous musicality, for it implies her uncomplicated closeness to the sources of music, nature and herself. The rudeness of peasant ways, the lack of circumspection and tact may also be what upset the well-spoken sisters who complain of her to the mother Abbess. When she arrives at the von Trapp mansion she is daunted but refuses to be over-impressed (as conveyed in Julie Andrews's performance); left alone in a great hall, she mocks aristocratic ways by bowing low and obsequiously. She refuses to let von Trapp's icy politeness freeze her out, doggedly speaks her mind and is not above sending him up. The spirit of peasant mockery of fine and fancy manners lingers in her. Yet she is also impressed by the grandeur of the household, the charm of the children, the name and tradition of the family. She may mock them, but she also respects them. She is pulled both ways.

Julie Andrews

An important inflection of the freedom/order opposition is carried, as a kind of sub-text, in the image and performance of Julie Andrews.

The Andrews image, which for some people is a reason for not going to see *The Sound of Music*, is made up basically of her roles in this film, *Mary Poppins* and the stage version of *My Fair Lady*. All subsequent appearances have been an attempt to break away from it. These three early roles have much in common, and the clear, bell-like, middle-class tones and jolly, awkward stance for which Andrews is often derided, are especially appropriate to them.

In terms of class, she plays characters of indeterminate or dubious class origin and ambiguous present position. In *My Fair Lady* she was archetypically a cockney lass. As Mary Poppins she was magic in origin – floating down from the sky, using an umbrella as a parachute. And Maria is a peasant girl, although peasant is a somewhat vague term, giving us no indication of wealth or occupation (farm labourer, tenant farmer, market gardener?). Maria's background is in fact still more indefinite by virtue of being an orphan, and then a novice. Each character enters a distinctly upper-class world – Eliza Doolittle passes herself off as belonging to it, something achieved above all through linguistic mastery; Mary and Maria are in a more ambiguous position – they are governesses. This is at once a servant job and a middle-class profession, although in Maria's case this latter has little meaning – she has had no training, has no job aspirations, in no way 'belongs' to a group of people which might be termed a profession. In none of these roles does Julie Andrews embody a middle-class type or view of the world, although all three are people who have gained entry to and acceptance in the upper reaches of society (royalty in *My Fair Lady*, aristocracy in *The Sound of Music*, banking upper-middle-class in *Mary Poppins*). In these contexts, the crisp and absolute precision of Julie Andrews's delivery has a certain edge to it, for it is the character's chief hold on acceptance.

In terms of sexuality, neither Mary Poppins nor Maria is free, uninhibited, sensual, although Eliza (at any rate so the number 'Show Me!' suggests) very probably is. The chimney sweep (Dick Van Dyke) who is in love with Mary implies that she is sexually inadequate – unfeeling, unable to respond, stiff. Maria on the other hand retreats to the abbey as soon as she begins to feel drawn to the Captain. The feelings confuse her, disorient her – she lacks as have women in this culture for over a century, any definition of or role for female sexuality. In this sense, then, Andrews's sexual awkwardness provides a kind of negative variation on the image of 'natural feeling' so positively affirmed in music. Once we have a definition of what freedom is like – here summed up in the numbers – we can embrace it joyously (hence the political importance of utopianism), but a freedom of feeling that knows no definition – as here with the female sexual impulse – is terrifying. Andrews as Maria *suffers* from just this aspect of the situation of women, and it provides a sombre possibility for audience identification that the film cannot really explore any further.

Section 2

The problems set up in the first part of the film are resolved in the second (i.e. from after 'The Lonely Goatherd' to the wedding of Maria and von Trapp) through the mediations of folk culture, and love and marriage. These represent the realization of Maria's aim – the unification of music and the world, of freedom and order.

Two of the turning-points in the narrative are based on folk culture – the song von Trapp is persuaded to sing, 'Edelweiss', and his dance, a Ländler with Maria during the ball. The use of folk idioms, melodies, dance forms to enrich the dominant tradition of culture has long been part of musical history – the nationalist movement in music was fundamentally based on it

– Grieg, Sibelius, Bartók, Dvořák, etc. – and the dance used here, the Ländler, is commonly supposed to have been the form from which the waltz was developed. Folk culture in this sense is the nexus of a form of nationalism, in which class distinctions melt and natural bonds are reasserted. The use of folk music, as opposed to the official written music, allows the dominant class to return to the people, to emphasize the common bond of a national heritage over and beyond present inequalities. Moreover, built into the idea of a return to the people is the idea of a return to nature, for the people, being less 'sophisticated', are held to be closer to nature and hence to the natural sources of music.

This is a romantic nationalism, basing itself in the culture of a peasantry declining in the face of industrialism and even in the qualities of the national geography (cf. *Song of Norway* where the music is shown to express the 'heart' of fjord scenery). It is also peculiarly apt, especially in musicals set in Europe, to unite the aristocracy and the peasantry, opposite but in some sense 'authentic' poles of the national culture, against the bureaucrats, the money-grubbers, or the spirit of the petty bourgeoisie incarnate in Nazism (cf. *Naughty Marietta, Call Me Madam, The Merry Widow, King's Rhapsody, Song of Norway*, etc.).

All this lies behind the use of respectable folk idioms in *The Sound of Music* – the song with its gentle, undemanding melody, its simple flower-as-emblem lyric; the dance, with its restrained formality and grace – as transition points for the breaking-down of the class barrier between Maria and the Captain, and in his conversion to music. Moreover, by introducing the nationalist element here, we are prepared for the final section of the film (the Germany/Austria confrontation).

Folk culture sets up a basis for understanding between Maria and von Trapp, but narrative expectations demand that this should issue in love and marriage. This duly happens, yet with an odd lack of conviction on the film's part, in the 'Something Good' number. This takes place in the summer-house, a setting already established as a locus of love by the number 'You Are Sixteen'. But where this number was bright and gay, culminating in a strutting and leaping dance choreographed to a thunderstorm and cymbal crashes, 'Something Good' is shot in misted focus, semi-darkness, with still-ness of movement in both performers and camera. One could say it embodies the characters' uncertainty and caution, yet it also effectively blurs their inter-action, as if Maria and von Trapp, and therefore freedom and order, are not, folk culture notwithstanding, really compatible. Thus the film manages to dissolve the contradictions and get us to the narrative resolution in marriage, but through the rather weak strategies of folk culture, a thinly realized love match and the spectacle of a wedding with baroque architecture and cathe-dral choir. Although the film now proceeds as if it had kicked over the trace of the earlier narrative tensions, they surface again, to be resolved only by the rather more stoic closing image.

Section 3

At this point, the film suddenly stops being a musical. There are no new numbers in the rest of the film, only reprises of 'Edelweiss' and 'Climb Every Mountain'. This is a pattern common in Rodgers and Hammerstein musicals: the climax of *The King and I* is the escape of Tup-Tim, her recapture, Anna's challenge to the King as he is about to whip the girl, and his collapse; the dénouement of *South Pacific* is a conventional war sequence, with one of the heroes bombed while on a spying mission. Similarly, *The Sound of Music* contains an exciting, but completely unmusical, climax of escape from Nazi patrols and over the border into Switzerland. What happens in each of these films is the growth and accomplishment of an understanding between the characters, which is then threatened by the intervention of a hostile country (Britain, Japan, Germany respectively) – the understanding is symbolized by an integration of music and narrative, so that the whole film becomes a musical world, which is then threatened and must be recovered by practical action. This narrative structure, with its strong emphasis on both interpersonal and patriotic loyalties, is in fact central to the intentions of Hammerstein, the librettist, who, as a member of the League of World Government, explicitly sought in the musicals to plead for tolerance towards other countries and their right to their own heritage and life-style (as expressed, of course, in their music or, ironically, Rodgers's Americanized version of it).

In the case of *The Sound of Music*, we have not only Germany threatening Austria, a straight nationalist threat, but another totalitarian regime, Nazism, which literally threatens musicality in its hostility to von Trapp's taking part in the Salzburg festival. But for this reworking of the freedom/order opposition, there is to be no magical resolution. The film ends with the family crossing the border over the mountains, the screen ringing with 'Climb Every Mountain'. This song was first introduced during Maria's temporary retreat to the abbey (where it is again shot with great formality, the Mother Abbess turning away into the shadow to begin it, and finally standing for the last verse with the stained-glass window lighting her beatifically). It fits in at the end in one sense simply because they are indeed climbing a mountain. Moreover, in its imagery the song takes up again the whole notion of human personality taking over nature, realizing the promise of background music. Facing up to life is seen as meeting the various obstacles that nature presents us with – mountains, streams, rainbows. . . . But by slipping into rainbow imagery, into the goal named as 'your dream', the song also hints at the fact that this is a never-ending quest, that life is a business of going on going on. And indeed this is where the film leaves it, not neat and tidy, for although the family has escaped the Germans, where have they really reached? We leave them climbing a mountain, not realizing a dream.

Conclusion

The Sound of Music takes as its point of departure real-life tensions, presented in an imaginative form – class relationships, sexual ambivalences and, centrally, the continuing contradiction between utter personal freedom and the social order of vested interests that is the enduring mark of bourgeois democracy. The film does not of course penetrate these contradictions to the realities of power and control, but rather presents the way the contradictions look and feel as they are lived. The film tries to offer easy ways out through the ideologies of nationalism and marriage, yet they are not brushed aside so lightly, and the film ends rather with a celebration of human endurance, the capacity to go on going on.

The Sound of Music takes this ending from both the musical and the 'woman's picture'. The happy ending commonly attributed to musicals is often, especially in later examples, of a fairly tough and bitter kind – think of *A Star is Born, Funny Girl, Gypsy, Sweet Charity, Cabaret*; and Rodgers and Hammerstein have made a feature of women's songs of endurance, self-sacrifice and hope – for instance, 'Climb Every Mountain', 'Something Wonderful' (*The King and I*), 'You'll Never Walk Alone' (*Carousel*), and, in lighter vein, 'A Cock-Eyed Optimist' (*South Pacific*). Similarly, the woman's picture in its weepie form, begins from a presentation of the double bind that women in society are faced with: the systematically contradictory roles that a woman is expected to inhabit – siren, paragon of virtue; wife (partner), mother (authority) and servant (looking after men). One of the ways out of this is simply to celebrate the capacity of the heroine to carry on in this impossible position: the genteel ability to cope of Greer Garson in *Mrs Miniver*, the determination and endurance of Joan Crawford in *Mildred Pierce*, the matriarchal control and self-sacrifice of Irene Dunne in *I Remember Mama* and so on. In *Gone with the Wind*, two types of this capacity are represented: Vivien Leigh's Scarlett, wilfulness becoming mature willpower, and Olivia de Havilland's Melanie, patient and enduring.

With its stylistic oppositions of music/order, with the determination of 'Confidence', the ability to find pleasure in small things ('My Favourite Things') and with the message of 'Climb Every Mountain', *The Sound of Music* goes directly into a world where women are caught between asserted individuality and strong pressures on role conformity, where much pleasure must be invested in trivial items, and where the horizons are such as let only endurance, the ability to go on, make immediate sense as a life-project. The question is whether it simply celebrates these attitudes, hence giving them a much-needed recognition and symbolic form, or else also locks its female audience more inexorably into trivia and endurance. But the Endurance of the People is one of the great socialist themes, and I don't see why we should disparage it just because it is in *The Sound of Music*.

Movie 23, 1976–7

8

SWEET CHARITY

A standard model for the history of a genre could be divided into three periods: primitive, mature and decadent. The first shows the genre in embryonic form, the second the full realization of its expressive potential and the third a reflective self-consciousness about the genre itself. If there is anything in this at all, then *Sweet Charity* represents the supreme achievement of the musical in its decadent period. It uses every trick in the cinematic book to embody the musical qualities of rhythm, melody and tone, and uses its total visual, aural and choreographic musicality to express a cynically wise view of the limitations of the musical genre.

The director Bob Fosse makes full use of the musical qualities of film – the rhythmic potential of editing, the melodic sweep of camera movement, the orchestral flair of colour and design. The cuts in 'If My Friends Could See Me Now' follow precisely the line of the song; the exact timing of the camera dolly that opens 'I'm a Brass Band' visualizes the exultant speed of the music.

Sweet Charity is full of such intoxicating effects, and yet they all go to produce a critique of 'the musical' which more than anything else suggests the hollowness of the genre's gospel of happiness. The story of most musicals is the pursuit and achievement of happiness, and in the classic examples the numbers are moments when happiness is achieved. *Sweet Charity* also follows this narrative pattern. Charity's story is a series of episodes, each of them an encounter with a potential source of happiness. But each of these sources lets her down, and the treatment of happiness in the musical numbers already expresses the emptiness of what is on offer, even before Charity realizes it herself.

There are four major areas of potential happiness in Charity's story – religion, love, entertainment and friendship. Religion is dealt with in only one number, 'The Rhythm of Life', where the lyrics of Sammy Davis Jr's wicked performance as Big Daddy, the busy colours of the believers' clothes and their crazed, cramped body-movements all mercilessly mock that type of organized religion, especially in its trendier forms.

Figure 8.1
Sweet Charity:
women for men

Figure 8.2
Sweet Charity: women
for themselves

Love is dealt with more kindly, but no more credulously. Three numbers mark Charity's relationship with Oscar: the first, 'It's a Nice Face', is half whispered to a prostrate Oscar after he has fainted in the lift – the feeling is very low-key; he sings the second, 'Sweet Charity' to her, their mutual exhilaration rendered 'unreal' by being shot in slow motion to emphasize what becomes evident immediately afterwards, that his love is based on his not knowing that she is a dance-hall hostess; and the third, Charity's 'I'm a Brass Band', sung when Oscar asks her to marry him despite what he now knows about her, is splendid but bizarre. Charity, dressed in a bright red uniform, dances around deserted New York streets like a majorette. She cries out 'Somebody loves me!' and a whole stadium of people roars approval. It is a delirium of love based, as is soon clear, on the quicksands of Oscar's hang-ups.

However, the most penetrating use of musical numbers is reserved for those set in places of entertainment – 'Big Spender' (Figure 8.1) in the dance-hall where Charity works, and the dances in the posh Pompeii club. Worlds apart socially, they are very similar choreographically – insistently sexual, yet in an angular, stiffened, ugly way that has nothing of sensuous enjoyment in it. 'If My Friends Could See Me Now' also refers to professional entertainment. Sung and danced by Charity, it expresses her jubilation at being in Vittorio Vitale's flat, and the musical form she instantly turns to is vaudeville, ending up with a spotlit hat-and-cane routine. She is really happy, but the movement is hectic, the cutting frantic, and in a final hallucinatory moment it is as if she is really on a stage – which is precisely how fragile her happiness is.

It is only with the treatment of friendship that the cynicism abates. The film only indicates *after* 'There's Gotta Be Something Better Than This' the futility of employment aspirations for hookers, and *after* 'I Love to Cry at Weddings' the futility of the institution of marriage. While they are on screen, both numbers feel straightforwardly happy. 'There's Gotta Be Something Better Than This' (Figure 8.2) uses a kind of vigorous movement more often associated with male dancers to express the solidarity and determination of the three women (MacLaine magnificently supported by Chita Rivera and Paula Kelly). 'I Love to Cry at Weddings' uses soft-shoe barbershop harmonies, streamers and confetti to evoke an old-fashioned community of well-wishing. Only with friends (not lovers), only where she works – the very places she so seldom really looks – are there glimmers of real happiness to be found.

The Movie 75, 1981

9

ACTION!

It must have been the way I was saying it. When people have asked me if I've seen any good films lately, I've replied, 'Oh, yes – *Speed*', and they've looked startled. It's as if I wasn't saying the title of a film but lapsing into some ill-understood subcultural jargon: 'Yeah, man – speed'. Perhaps I lengthened the vowel or arched my body involuntarily, because they weren't entirely wrong. *Speed* is, like, speed.

In all truth, it isn't as much of a trip as one could imagine it being. There's nothing in it like the camera hanging out of the jeep in *Hatari!* or skimming over Julie Andrews in *The Sound of Music* or hand-held prowling in *Wolfen*, none of the magnificent shock cuts and zooms of Hammer horror or the likes of Mario Bava and Dario Argento, let alone the thrillingly torrential cutting of the Odessa steps sequence in *Battleship Potemkin* or the eponymous tempest in *Storm Over Asia*. Nor is there the gross-out factor in *Speed* that might elevate it to late night and video cult status, none of the gore of even a mainstream movie like *Under Siege* (kitchen knives in skulls, fingers in eyeballs), to say nothing of the I-can't-believe-I'm-seeing-this climaxes of films like *Basket Case* or *The Re-animator* (but don't bother to check this out on the British release videos). Indeed, *Speed* teasingly draws back from delivering such an experience, even when it titillates us with the promise that it's about to show us a white, middle-class mother and baby smashed to smithereens.

Speed gets its rush from a sheer squandering of sensational situations. Keanu Reeves is a cop who has to deal with three desperate predicaments: a plummeting lift, a bus primed to explode if it drops to below 50 m.p.h. and an out-of-control subway train. One follows straight after the other, set in motion by an obscurely vengeful ex-cop (Dennis Hopper) with a genius for deadly remote control technology. Any one of these variations on velocity would have been enough for most movies. *Speed* is like Sylvester Stallone dangling over the ravine at the start of *Cliffhanger* plus the office explosion in *Lethal Weapon 3* plus the train crash in *The Fugitive* plus the chase along the sunken canal in *Terminator 2*, all put end to end with no boring bits in between. No dodgy politics. No naff attempts at psychologizing the villain he's a nutcase. No mushy buddiness: the film barely pauses when Keanu's partner is blown to bits through Keanu's lack of foresight. No elaborate excuses to get the camera to linger on the star's muscles: Keanu's not that kind of boy. And no love interest to send the kids into frenzies of squabbling and going to the loo: there is a girl (in fact, Sandra Bullock on fine form) and Keanu does get her, but it's all done on the run with only a quick clinch at the end. This is the movie as rollercoaster: all action and next to no plot.

The cinema has always had the potential to be like this. Whether it is really true that the first audiences for the Lumière brothers' film of a train entering a station did duck in terror as it advanced towards them, the idea that they did has often seemed to be emblematic of what film is all about. The Lumières ushered in a new technology, that has become ever more elaborate, revelling in both showing and creating the sensation of movement. *Train Entering a Station* and *Speed* belong to a distinguished lineage. It includes all those celebrations of movement so prized by earlier commentators on film: the simple documentary dwelling on movement, be it on the vast or tiny, train crashes or water fleas (to take oft-cited very early examples); such staged delights as the Keystone Cops, cowboys and indians, Fred and Ginger, climaxes à la Griffith; and all those attempts to make cinema move analogously to music: animated abstract ballets, 'symphonies' of the great modern cities. The lineage also includes, however, *This is Cinerama*, Imax cinema presentations and the Showscan Dynamic Motion Simulator, a 'magic chair' that promised to deliver 'the ultimate fantasy: Reality'. The celebration of sensational movement, that we respond to in some still unclear sense 'as if real', for many people is the movies.

I would not want to erect this into an absolute aesthetic principle, as some film theorists and critics have done. The stasis of filmmakers such as Ozu, Duras and Akerman is just as tonic and authentically cinematic as the movement of Murnau, Minnelli or, indeed, Jan De Bont, the director of *Speed*. Yet stillness and contemplation are rare in popular cinema. The triumph of the word 'movie' over the more static 'pictures' or wonderfully evocative 'flicks' is not just a product of US cultural imperialism; it also catches something of the sensation we expect when we go to the cinema.

It seems, though, that we seldom want the sense of movement and excitement, the speed, by itself. How many times does one want to visit the Imax or a Showscan Dynamic Motion Simulator? We generally want the exhilaration and rush embedded in a fiction. Such fictions situate the thrills. They refer us to the world. They do not usually pretend to show us the world as it really is, but they point to that world. They offer us thrills and elations we might seldom have, might think it impossible really to have, but they relate such imaginings of elation to the human coordinates of the real world: the environments we live in, the social categories in which we have our being. In the process, they propose and legitimate kinds of thrills, and who gets them and who pays the price.

In contemporary cinema, it is the action film that most characteristically delivers speed in a story. One has only to think of the stars of such films – Schwarzenegger, Stallone, Bruce Willis, Harrison Ford, Steven Seagal, Jean Claude van Damme, and now Keanu Reeves – to have an indication of whose thrills are being legitimated: straight white men. This doesn't mean that no one else can possibly imagine having the thrills alongside Arnie or Keanu, but it does contribute to the reproduction of a masculine structure of feeling. Extreme sensation is represented as experienced not within the body but in the body's contact with the world, its rush, its expansiveness, its physical stress and challenge, and this is seen as essentially male. There is nothing wrong with such feelings of extreme and, as it were, worldly sensation, but the movies tie it to male characters and male environments, suggesting it is really only appropriate to men. This is not a matter of saying that I want – let alone of my wanting women to want – to have quite this kind of sensational experience, but that there is a deeper, underlying pattern of feeling, to do with freedom of movement, confidence in the body, engagement with the material world, that is coded as male (and straight and white, too) but to which all humans need access.

In *Speed*, as in most action films of the past fifteen or more years, it is not quite true to say that *only* straight, white men get the thrills. We now have a well-established pattern, whereby the hero is accompanied by white women and men of colour (rarely women of colour) who are also exposed to the dangers that bring the thrills. Though the screaming heroine or cringing black man who are more hindrance than help do still crop up, women and men of colour are nowadays more likely to be allowed to be tough and brave, to be able handle themselves and often to have skills the white hero doesn't possess. Even if they don't start out that way, they eventually make the grade. The figure of the black police chief or crack platoon leader who provides support and back-up at crucial moments is a staple of the genre, as is the moment when the heroine finally has to kill, deliberately and efficiently, to save the cornered hero.

Speed loses its potential black helper, the bus driver in the central segment, early on, leaving Keanu and his white helper to save the busload of mainly non-white passengers. The white helper, though, is a woman, Sandra Bullock. Unlike her (literally) poor fellow commuters, she's only travelling by bus because she has had her driving licence taken away for speeding (the film is not without a sense of humour). She has to take charge of the bus when the driver is incapacitated and performs brilliantly, managing sharp corners and interweaving across busy traffic lanes, all at top speed, with splendid aplomb and verve mixed with terror. She does get the thrills of extreme physical danger and the exultation of mastery of a machine. Yet *Speed* still conforms to the pattern of contemporary action films by constituting her as helper. She's not the main man. Conan (in the Schwarzenegger films) and Indiana Jones are two of the many heroes who now do their thing with women and black people in tow, but never quite as equals, never with quite the same access to the speed of worldly sensation.

Worldly thrills are seldom bought at no price. In the classic Western and jungle adventure film, to take relatively easy targets, it is the native people who pay the biggest price for the white man's exhilaration. With Rambo or a film like *Under Siege*, it's anyone who gets in the way, which generally means other males – many action films are indeed mainly affairs between men. *Speed* largely avoids giving us time to note death: there are innocent bystanders knocked off and some police, but by and large *Speed* is oddly benign. Old ladies petrified to leap from lifts, babies in prams, poor commuters of colour on the unstoppable bus, such people are safe with *Speed*, not expendable as they might be in many other films. The price is elsewhere, in things. It is the transport system itself that is smashed about, cars, lorries, barriers, planes and even the roadway itself in a final eruption of a subway train from below. It is an orgy of destruction of one of the great frustrations of modern urban living, getting about.

It is not impossible to imagine action movies otherwise. They don't have to be about the destruction of subject peoples and the natural environment, they don't have to centre forever on straight white men. The shifts in gender and race roles that I've already suggested indicate the possibility of change. The problem with *Passenger 57* (which in any case was no worse than *Under Siege*, say, or *Die Hard 2*) was not that its hero was a black man, and certainly not Wesley Snipes's adequacy as a star, but dull plotting and direction. There are many precedents for the woman as hero of adventure, notably Leni Riefenstahl's mountain films, Fearless Nadia (the Indian star celebrated in the film *Fearless: The Hunterwali Story*), Sigourney Weaver in the *Alien* films, and the 'women warriors' discussed by Yvonne Tasker with characteristic flair in her *Spectacular Bodies* (1993).

Yet I would not want to underestimate how difficult it will be to make it normal and unremarkable to have people of colour and women as the subject of worldly sensation. Experience of space has race and gender dimensions which set limits to how plausible or excessively exceptional one may find a representation. Colour ghettoization, for instance, instils assumptions about space that are hard to shake. White people often say they are fearful of going into black ghettos, but seldom stop to consider that such ghettos are themselves surrounded on all sides by the powerful white ghetto. Entering and being in white space can be profoundly intimidating, however astonishingly at ease Wesley Snipes or Danny Glover may appear in it on screen. Even more fundamentally, perhaps, much cross-cultural research suggests that we start learning our relation to our environment from the moment of cradling, and that we learn it differently according to gender. To feel that it is OK to be unrestrained, to kick against what surrounds you, to thrust out into the world is what boys learn, not girls. To see women strain against the world may be inspirational but also at some psychic level unbelievable.

Heroes of action who are other than male and white (and straight and able bodied) are still going to feel exceptional for some time to come.

To summarize: action movies, as the most common contemporary form of the cinema of sensation, ally the speed they offer with white male characters and a white masculine structure of feeling. Women and people of colour may be let in on the action, but either in secondary roles or with a strong sense of their exceptionality. Yet the experience which action movies offer is in another way not so very traditionally masculine at all.

To go to an action movie is to sink back in the seat and say, 'show me a good time'. Maybe we also cringe, shield our eyes, convulse our bodies – maybe we are often not so much more sophisticated than those putative Lumière audiences – but mentally we abandon ourselves to the illusion. Many have seen this as the essence of nearly all film experience, no matter what the genre; it underlies the notion of 'classical cinema' that has become so entrenched in film studies. Such surrender to pleasure has greatly worried cultural, and not just film, criticism.

Perhaps the image that most famously captures this intellectual worry about movies as sensation is that of the feelies in Aldous Huxley's *Brave New World* : the masses hooked up to a wash of sensations as part of an enforced passivity that keeps them mindlessly turning the cogs of capitalism. There is a point here. Passivity in life, in politics, is problematic: it means acquiescing to a status quo that damages people along class, gender, racial, sexual and other lines; for many women lying back within actual heterosexual sex has not always meant enjoying it; and there are besides always others who pay the real price for the comforts and megabuck sensations of the world's well-to-do minority. Yet it is hard not see in Huxley's hatred something else: a libidinal fear of passivity itself.

Modern discussion of cultural pleasures tends to take sexuality as the founding form of all enjoyment, as the appetite *par excellence*. (I look forward to a return to theory and criticism which takes eating as its primary metaphor for understanding enjoyment.) Pleasures that are approved or disapproved of get mapped onto ideas of what sex is like. The notions of active and passive have been made to do a great deal of muddled but suggestive work ineluctably correlated with gender roles within heterosexuality. On the one hand, proper gender identity has seemed to be realized in the performance of active male and passive female coital roles. On the other hand, a phantasm of sex as assault has haunted the minds of heterosexual male intellectuals. As a result, when they have imagined passivity in sex they have imagined something terrifying. Passivity is thus both demeaning for a man because it makes him like a woman, and frightening too. So it is with all delectation – since sex provides the measure of all pleasures. The worst thing imaginable is to go to the cinema to lie back and enjoy it. Which suggests another terror, lurking beneath the fear of being like, and being treated like, a woman. For what kind of a man is it who lies back and does enjoy it? A queer, of course. Queers of every sex know that passivity need not be alarming, but then that's queers for you, not a palatable message for chaps hell bent on being straight.

In relation to adventure movies, there is a delicious paradox here. Such movies promote an active engagement with the world, going out into it, doing to the environment; yet enjoyment of them means allowing them to come to you, take you over, do you. When Jean-Claude van Damme kicks his way out of trouble, when Harrison Ford leaps into the torrent in *The Fugitive* (as Butch and Sundance did before him), when Keanu lies on his back under the careering bus in *Speed*, we may identify with them, imagine the rush of excitement as we brace ourselves against, and master, the world; but we're also letting ourselves be carried along, going with the flow of the movie, ecstatically manipulated.

The favoured position of hard-core fans for watching action movies in the cinema is slumped in the seat with legs slung over the seat in front. This is an excellent position for anal sex as well as for cunnilingus and fellatio. Come to think of it, for the male viewer action movies have a lot in common with being fellated. At the level of cultural imagery, the fellatee is considered the butch one – perhaps because he supplies the phallus in the transaction, perhaps because fellatio facilitates a masculine dissociation of mind and body more readily than face to face coital positions. Whatever the reason, men cherish the illusion that their masculinity is not compromised by being fellated. Yet it's the other person, male or female, who's really doing all the work, really being active. So it is with action movies. In imagination, men can be Arnie or Keanu; but in the seat, it's Arnie or Keanu pleasuring them. Now that's what I call speed.

Sight and Sound 4 (10) (NS), 1994

Reference

Tasker, Yvonne (1993) *Spectacular Bodies: Gender, Genre and the Action Cinema*, London: Routledge.

Further reading

Arroyo, José (ed.) (2000) *Action/Spectacle Cinema*, London: British Film Institute.
Dyer, Richard (1997) 'The white man's muscles', in *White*, London: Routledge, 145–83.

10

LETHAL REPETITION

Serial killers kill serially: one murder after another, each a variation and continuation of the ones before and the ones to follow, each an episode in the serial. Then, the police and the media identify a number of apparently disconnected murders as in fact a connected sequence and the logic of seriality unfolds: the discovery of further corpses, the next instalments in the killing, the investigation, the culprit's apprehension, trial and even their life in prison. In turn, each killer is fitted into the yet wider serial of serial killing itself, with its stars, fact, fiction or both (Jack the Ripper, the vampire of Düsseldorf, Henri Landru and M. Verdoux, Norman Bates, Ian and Myra, Jeffrey Dahmer, Hannibal the Cannibal, the Wests) and its featured players, the police, victims, witnesses and acquaintances. And then there are television serials about serial killers: *Millennium*, *Touching Evil*, *Headless*, *Serial Killers*.

There were television serial killers before these. Several of the star real-life serial killers have had mini-series devoted to them, provided their tendencies were not too gross to be accommodated within television's 'family audience' remit. Thus we had Ted Bundy, the all-American guy so clean cut he could talk himself into any young woman's company (*The Deliberate Stranger*, 1986) and Ted Gacy, respectable citizen and murderer of boys galore (*To Catch a Killer*, 1992), but not Ed Gein, whose human skin draping inspired *Psycho* (1960), *The Texas Chainsaw Massacre* (1974), *Deranged* (1974), *The Silence of the Lambs* (1991) and finally *Ed Gein* (2000), but nothing made for television, nor yet Jeffrey Dahmer's charnel house or the Wests' prolonged molestation, torture and incest. Serial killers have featured in most police and detective series; the first episodes of two series sold on the novelty of having women detective heroes, *Cagney and Lacey* (1982) and *Prime Suspect* (1991), dealt with serial killers, while the first series of *Band of Gold* (1995) dealt with a group of prostitutes who came together under the threat of a serial killer; there have even been serial killers in episodes of *Earth: Final Conflict*, *Fantasy Island* and *Star Trek* ('Wolf to the Fold' 1967).

Nonetheless, before *Millennium* there was probably only one television serial posited on serial killing, *Kolchak: The Night Stalker* (1974–5), and its multiple murderers were vampires, mad scientists, werewolves and witches, never natural born men. Now (1995–2001), however, television is packed with serial killers. I have lost track of all their appearances in television series and made-for-TV movies (e.g. *Vegas Vice* (1994), *A Feel for Murder* (1995), *Falling For You* (1995), *Prescription for Murder* (1995), *Profile for Murder* (1996), *Scene of the Crime* (1996), *Sealed with a Kiss* (1996), *Intensity* (1997), *Bone Daddy* (1998), *Perfect Prey* (1998), *Mind Games* (2001)). Serial killers are a classic television phenomenon. They feed off the huge commercial and critically approved wave of serial killing best-sellers and movies: Michael Connelly, Patricia Cornwell, Thomas Harris, Val McDermid; *The Silence of the Lambs*, *Seven* (1995), *Hannibal* (2001); and, because they have a superb inbuilt narrative hook – when's the next one? – they are perfect for carrying viewers over ad and episode breaks.

Real serial killing was named in the 1970s after the film serials of the 1940s and 1950s. Robert Ressler, one of the first criminal profilers for the Federal Bureau of Investigation (FBI), told an interviewer that he saw such killing as 'distinctly episodic, like the movie-house serials he enjoyed as a boy' (Michaud 1986: 41).[1] That act of naming provides a grim insight into the construction of real and fictional serial killing, for both are ineluctably tied to the pleasure principle of seriality.

This has deep roots. Bards, jongleurs, griots and yarn spinners, to say nothing of parents and nurses, have all long known the value of leaving their listeners wanting more, of playing on that mix of repetition and anticipation, and indeed of the anticipation of repetition, that underpins serial pleasure. However it is only under capitalism that seriality becomes a reigning principle of cultural production, first in novel and cartoon serialization, then in the organization of news and movie programming. Its value as a selling device for papers and broadcasts is obvious. Consider the murder of Gianni Versace in 1996 (filmed as *The Versace Murder*, 1997), which became an even better news story with the suggestion that the killer was a serial one. Each day sold news of fresh revelations and speculations – the killer wore dresses, maybe the Mafia was involved, had the suspect been seen at a party at Gianni's only a week before? – to the point that the alleged killer's suicide seemed almost spoilsporting, bringing a good story to so swift a conclusion. And the apotheosis of seriality as a principle is television, constantly interweaving serial strands, the orchestration of which is known as scheduling.

Serial killing is often taken to be the crime of our age. It is held to be facilitated by the anonymity of mass societies and the ease and rapidity of modern transport, to be bred from the dissolution of the affective bonds of community and lifelong families, and fomented by the routinization of the sexual objectification of women in the media. It is supposedly a symptom of a society in which worth is judged in terms of fame, to the point that spectacularly terrible killing is just a route to celebrity. Whether actual serial

71

killing, in any case a less unified phenomenon than the myth of the serial killer makes it appear, does characterize our times or not, it certainly does articulate many of these perceptions of what makes our times our times. To this we must add seriality.

Towards the beginning of *M* (1931), we see the murder of little Elsie, the film's first. Haunting images signifying her death – her ball rolling to a stop amid patches of grass, her balloon man caught up in telegraph wires – are followed by a black screen; then out of the silence emerges the sound of a newspaper seller calling out 'Extra! Another murder!' over and over again; the scene fades up, and his slowish, regular repetition is augmented by the shriller, faster, more irregular voices of boy sellers running along the street, which is swiftly thronged with people jostling to buy the papers. Even before this a capella celebration of seriality, we have seen children at the beginning of the film playing a counting game in which, one by one, serially, the players are 'eliminated'. We see Elsie bouncing a ball against a poster proclaiming that 'The Murderer Is Among Us', clearly a message endlessly repeated throughout the city. Then her mother, anxious that she is so late getting home, goes with relief to answer a ring at the door, only to find a man delivering 'a sensational new chapter' of some story to which she subscribes. The Düsseldorf of *M* is awash with macabre seriality, intensified by the horror and prurience evinced by child sexual killing.

Seriality emphasizes anticipation, suspense: What will happen next? It also emphasizes repetition, pattern, structure. We may enjoy the excitement of the threat posed by a serial killer – when will he strike next and whom? when will they get him? – but we can also enjoy discerning the pattern in his acts. This may be the same basic pattern in each act – the same selection of victim, the same method of killing – or it may be the way that a pattern emerges out of all the killing seen as a sequence. The commonest form of the first kind of pattern is explanation – each act becomes an expression of the same underlying pattern of motivation. A classic example of the second kind of pattern – that virtually only exists in fiction – would be a series of killings based upon some numerical or alphabetical sequence.

Two films from 1995, *Seven* and *Copycat*, play on the pleasure of discerning pattern in serial killing. In the first, we share the realization by Somerset (Morgan Freeman) that apparently disconnected murders are connected and later that the connection enacts the seven deadly sins. The elegant simplicity of the design is underscored by the use of titles for each successive day of the week, indicating that there will be seven sins in seven days, and intensified by having each sinner killed by means of his or her own sin (the glutton forced to eat till his stomach bursts, the woman of lust literally fucked to death by a dildo in the form of a serrated knife and so on). We await – almost certainly eagerly, or else why do we stay? – the discovery of the next atrocity. The beauty of the structure lies in the way it draws both the killer John Doe (Kevin Spacey) and Mills (Brad Pitt), the other investigating officer into the chain of murders so that the whole structure folds back on itself. Doe is killed for his envy, Mills's career and mind are destroyed by his wrath. What's more, both effect this destruction on each other, Doe goading Mills into killing him (Doe), knowing that this will destroy Mills. No narrative knot was ever more elegantly tightened.

Copycat also develops an exquisitely simple pattern into which killer and investigators are woven. Like the serial killer expert Helen (Sigourney Weaver) and cop M.J. (Holly Hunter), we come to recognize the broad principle of the killing repetitions, each being based on the *modus operandi* of a previous celebrated killer. But the order in which these imitative murders are undertaken is a problem, for it is not chronological, say, or alphabetical. Only near the end does Helen realize that they follow the order these star killers were listed in a lecture she gave – and we saw – at the film's start. As the investigator, she discerns a pattern she herself supplied in the first place. A frightening logic ensures. After her lecture, she had been menaced by serial killer Darryl Lee Cullum (Harry Connick Jnr), only narrowly escaping death. The copycat killer wants now to round off this unfinished pattern, to make a perfect series of killings by repeating Darryl Lee's attack. The film, however, wants to repeat *itself*, so this killing too must only be an attempted one, bringing the film to a perfect formal closure.

Not all serial killer films offer such dispassionate pleasures. A slasher movie like *The Texas Chainsaw Massacre* is so remorselessly visceral that one hardly has time to sit back and discern patterns. Some films even deliberately upset the desire to savour structures. Henry (Michael Rooker) of *Henry: Portrait of a Serial Killer* (1986/1990) is versed in serial killer discourse and knows that he will be caught if he repeats himself in his murders; this is one of the basic tenets with which he inducts Otis (Tom Towles) into killing. Yet the denial of distinctive form to the killing only emphasizes the sheer repetitiveness of it – no clever, even witty patterns, just on and on and on. The film opens with a series of long takes, intercutting dead female bodies and Henry having breakfast or driving about. We inevitably connect the two elements, assume the bodies are Henry's victims, but we're never told they are connected at all, let alone that these are his first victims. Henry's killing thus has no beginning and nor is it separable from the regularity of random slaughter across America. And if there's no beginning, there's no end. The film finishes with Henry dumping a suitcase with, presumably, a body in it, probably the girl he might have settled down with; but the film then stops, with no sense that Henry's killing has come to an end.

Where there is no beginning or end there can be no pattern, and this is reinforced in *Henry* by the absolute refusal to give explanations for what he does, no behavioural deviance (as in *M*), no woman blaming (*Psycho*), no childhood trauma (*Tenebre*, 1982), no media infection (*Natural Born Killers*, 1994), just endless slaughter. *Kalifornia* (1993) likewise upsets the hope that serial killing has a pattern and serial killers an explanation. As writer and photographer respectively, Brian and Carrie (David Duchovny and Michelle Forbes) set off across America visiting the sites of famous murders, aiming to produce a glossy book of entertainment and explanation. Through an advertisement, they take on Early and Adele (Brad Pitt and Juliette Lewis) to share the costs of the journey. But Early is a killer and, since he kills repeatedly, he could be termed a serial killer – except he does it mainly out of convenience. He doesn't kill for the sake of it, let alone to enact the elegant patterns of *Seven* or *Copycat*. When he has no money for petrol at a garage, he simply kills a man in the toilet and steals from him to pay the bill. Though the film is less interesting than it sounds, the premise – that serial killing is just a lot of killing done for different, practical reasons by the same person – subverts the longing for form and sense that *Seven* and *Copycat* so amply satisfy.

For all *Seven*'s stunning bleakness, its assertion of a pattern to its killings seems reassuring beside *Henry*'s vision of killing without shape or sense. Both *Seven* and *Copycat* are actually rather old-fashioned works, finished and self-contained. *Henry* is more truly modern, more like television. It realizes, in macabre and terrible form, the quintessence of seriality, the soap opera, the story with no beginning and no end. *Seven* and *Copycat* give us the feeling that we can sit back in the dark, see the pattern and make sense of it, however appalling. With *Henry*, there is no such sense – it opens up the spectre of endlessness, forever trapped by the compulsions of serial watching, engulfed in repetition without end or point.

Not that the compulsive repetitions of serial killing are random. Though such classy works as *Manhunter* (1986), *Seven*, *Millennium* and *Hannibal* avoid the issue, serial killers – in fact and in fiction – are not just people who kill people; they are men who kill women or socially inferior men (boys, blacks, queers). The numbers of women or non-white men who are serial killers are so tiny as to be statistically negligible, as are the number of grown, heterosexual, white men who are victims (leaving aside the few who are killed because they get in the way).

Serial killer fictions condemn the slaughter of women, of course, but they also provide opportunities for misogyny. One commanding pattern of explanation for the killer's behaviour is to blame it on women: dominating and teasing mothers, provocative flirts, prostitutes as the repository of male sexual disgust. Typically, two of Hitchcock's serial killer films play with the blaming of women for femicide. *Psycho* has the psychiatrist at the end explain that Norman (Anthony Perkins) was over-possessed and humiliated by his mother as a child, producing a morbid inability to relate normally to other women; by the end of his exposition, he slides from suggesting that Norman has produced the character of his mother in his own head to saying that really he is his mother and that it was she who slew Marion Crane (Janet Leigh) and was responsible for a few other unsolved murders in the neighbourhood. At the end of the film, for a split second, we see Mrs Bates's skull looking up out of

74

Norman's grinning face. We could take all this as evidence of Hitchcock's misogyny, were it not offset by the neat banality and tedious theatrics of the psychiatrist and the ambiguity of Norman's grin, perhaps signalling awareness of having put one over on the credulous expert. *Frenzy* (1972) is yet more disturbing in its toying with misogyny. Throughout the film we are asked to feel the frightfulness of women, from the snobbery and humiliation heaped on Richard (Jon Finch) by his ex-wife Brenda (Barbara Leigh-Hunt) to the ghastly meals served up to Inspector Oxford (Alec McCowen) by his wife (Vivienne Merchant). The film encourages misogyny, only, in the utter ugliness of the way it shows the murders, to show us the logical conclusion of such feelings and rap us over the knuckles for having felt them. All this is brilliantly done and morally complex – but you could just feel that *Psycho* is a film about how women fuck up men and take *Frenzy* as an opportunity to enjoy some really ugly and emotionally justified women killing.

Nor in their condemnation of slaughter do serial killing movies often eschew the sadistic visual pleasure of a camera bearing down on a cowering woman. The horrible *Maniac* (1980) contains one of the most unspeakably protracted scenes of suspense in all movies, with a victim huddling terrified in a cubicle in a deserted women's toilet in the notoriously dangerous New York subway as the killer stalks her. Are we to identify with her and her terror, either in order to remember just how terrible serial killing is, or else to experience fear vicariously, as a masochistic thrill? Or are we simply to enjoy watching her suffer? And who does the film think 'we' are, men or women?

Serial killers may be horrific, but at the same time they may be figures to be identified with. They are often hero or cult figures, from Jack the Ripper to Freddy Kruger, and real-life serial killers receive stacks of devoted fan mail (as does Darryl Lee in *Copycat*). Not for nothing has the third of Thomas Harris's serial killer novels (and the films based on them) acknowledged that their real hero is the killer not the detective, heroic not just in the sense of being their centre, as the title *Hannibal* indicates, but even the embodiment of values and, at the end of the last film, self-sacrifice over against the petty careerism of the FBI.

The misogyny within serial killer identification or admiration may be quite explicit woman-hating, dwelling and getting off on the killer's dominance and destruction of women, or it may be more displaced, a fascination with his power, even his genius. Lecter does not verbally express hatred of women, is courteous to Clarice and does not primarily kill women, yet his whole persona, and not least his ineffable sarcasm, is founded on the supremacy of the powerful and the expendability of the weak, a glorification that sits easily with notions of white masculinity. Not the least of the genius of the killer in classy films is an ability to discipline a murderous tendency into witty serial patterns.

Though women are central to the serial killer phenomenon, the *raison d'être* for killer and investigator alike, much of the actual action in a serial killer fiction is between men, on-screen between killer and pursuer and also to a considerable extent between screen and audience. And along with their misogynist pleasures, they also tend to posit men as the only possible saviours of women.

Police detection as such is often shown to be feeble. It is the chance sharing of a lift between the detectives and Albert De Salvo, arrested for house-breaking, that lead the former to identify the latter as *The Boston Strangler* (1968), while John Doe simply gives himself up in *Seven*. Where they don't rely on chance, investigators often rely on criminals. The underworld gets to the child killer of *M* before the police, Clarice depends on Lecter's wisdom to track down Buffalo Bill in *The Silence of the Lambs*.

There is one exception to all this rather shaky detection: the profiler, the genius-like investigator who, on the basis of clues at the scene of the crime, is able to narrow down the social and geographical location of the killer as well as his psychological make-up. This figure has echoes of Sherlock Holmes who has indeed been pressed into service in the hunt for Jack the Ripper in *A Study in Terror* (1965) and *Murder by Decree* (1979). However, the real-life models are Robert Ressler, who advised Thomas Harris on *Red Dragon* (filmed as *Manhunter*) and *The Silence of the Lambs*, and John Douglas, head of the FBI's National Center for the Analysis of Violent Crime, whose watchword – to know the criminal, one must study his crime – is pure Holmes. Stories about profilers suggest almost preternatural powers. Douglas recounts the example of a psychiatrist James Brussel, used by the police in the investigation of the 'Mad Bomber' (active in and around New York between 1940 and his capture in 1957); Dr Brussel's profile of the killer was accurate in every detail (in his early fifties, of Slavic origin, living in Bridgeport Connecticut and wearing double-breasted suits that he always kept buttoned up). Such astounding ratiocination became in *Millennium* an extrasensory gift whereby flashing visions lead Frank Black (Lance Hendriksen) to the week's culprit. *Citizen X* (1995), a television movie on the Soviet killer Andrei Chikatilo, is much more sober yet still draws on the idea of special intellectual powers: detective Viktor Burakov (Stephen Rea) unerringly deduces on the flimsiest evidence that the killer picks up his victims at train stations and just knows which such casual pick-up of the many he observes is the killer in action; later, the pyschiatrist Alexander Kravchenko (Max Von Sydow) reads out to Chikatilo (Jeffrey DeMunn) his report on him (based only on the evidence of the crimes), and so uncannily accurate is it, so utterly does Chikatilo feel himself known, that he at once confesses after days of resisting police grilling.

Manhunter, *Seven* and *Millennium* all emphasize the home life of the detective. Just as in the Western and gangster film, home is the realm of normal reproductive sexuality at stake in the hero's engagement with the killer's abnormal, destructive world. He is protecting home from what the killer represents, doing his bit to make the world safe for women and children. Th potential invasion of the home is the deepest anxiety in Hitchcock's *Shadow of a Doubt* (1941) and in *Manhunter* and *Millennium* (where it provided a running weekly cliff-hanger); and it is brought to devastating fruition in *Seven*.

In this context – of men killing women and of men pursuing men in the name of women – *Copycat* is a surprising film. Other films (*Basic Instinct* (1992), *Butterfly Kiss* (1995) and every other Italian giallo) aim to surprise by flying in the face of statistics and featuring female serial killers. But *Copycat*'s opening scene has Helen underline in her lecture the fact that serial killers are overwhelmingly white and male. This moment counters two of the mainstays of serial killer movies. First, it insists that the killers are (in all other respects) typical white men, not exceptional monsters; second, it is a woman who demonstrates this, with all the authority of expertise.

Another woman, M.J., then joins forces with Helen, to track down and destroy the copycat killer. The obvious predecessor, Clarice in *The Silence of the Lambs*, has to turn to a male expert, Lecter, to help her, and by the time of *Hannibal* this has turned into a kind of naff romance. Detective M.J., however, not only turns to a female and non-criminal expert, Helen, but in her first scene in the film, is shown to be more able to handle herself physically than her hunky male sidekick. Moreover, he is eliminated towards the film's end, leaving Sigourney and Holly alone to face the killer. Nor is it masculine-style heroics that destroy this killer, but instead female derision. When it seems that there is no way out for her, that the killer has her in his power, Helen just starts to laugh at the absurdity of it all – and it is the killer's confusion and dismay at this that unmans him, leaving the way open for M.J. to shoot him.

Why does Helen laugh? Perhaps a kind of hysteria, or relief that now her life of anxiety will be ended. But also perhaps because she sees the profound absurdity of the seriousness with which men take serial killing. The destruction of others, the lethal pursuit of women, is of course serious. But when it gets dressed up in all these clever patterns (*Seven*, *Copycat* itself), or gets passed off as genius (Lecter), it is also appallingly silly. *Seven*'s bleakness is sublime, a symphony of despair, but the end of *Copycat* accords with *Henry*: killing is just killing is just killing.

Sight and Sound 7 (9) (NS), 1997 (revised)

Note

1   Michael Newton (2000: 205) disputes Ressler's claim to be the original coiner of the term.

References

Michaud, Stephen G (1986) 'The FBI's new psyche squad', *New York Times* (magazine) 26 October, 40–41.

Newton, Michael (2000) *The Encyclopedia of Serial Killers*, New York: Checkmark Books.

Further reading

Black, Joel (1991) *The Aesthetics of Murder: A Study in Romantic Literature and Contemporary Culture*, Baltimore, MD: Johns Hopkins University Press.

Cameron, Deborah and Frazer, Elizabeth (1987) *The Lust to Kill*, London: Polity.

Clover, Carol (1992) *Men, Women and Chainsaws*, London: British Film Institute.

Conrath, Robert (1994) 'The guys who shoot to thrill: serial killers and the American popular unconscious', *Revue française d'études américaines* 60, 143–52.

Coursodon, Jean-Pierre (1996) 'Du meurtre en série considéré comme un des beaux-arts', *Positif* 420, 87–91.

Hart, Lynda (1994) *Fatal Women*, London: Routledge.

Kaes, Anton (2000) *M*, London: British Film Institute.

Menarini, Roy (1996) 'I serial killer movies: l'antieroe postmoderno', *Segnocinema* 16 (82), 7–9.

Musci, Aldo, Alessandro Scarso and Giuseppe Tavella (eds) (1997) *Vivere per uccidere: Serial Killer, Mass-murder, Family Murder, Ritual Murder*, Padua: Calusca.

Nixon, Nicola (1998) 'Making monsters, or serializing killers', in Martin, Robert K. and Savoy, Eric (eds) *American Gothic: New Interventions in a National Narrative*, Iowa City, IA: University of Iowa Press, 217–36.

Pinedo, Isabel Cristina (1997) *Recreational Terror: Women and the Pleasures of Horror Film Viewing*, Albany, NY: State University of New York Press.

Sharrett, Christopher (ed.) (1999) *Mythologies of Violence in Postmodern Media*, Detroit, IL: Wayne State University Press.

Tatar, Maria (1995) *Lustmord: Sexual Murder in Weimar Germany*, Princeton, NJ: Princeton University Press.

Taubin, Amy (1994) 'Grabbing the knife: *The Silence of the Lambs* and the history of the serial killer movie' in Cook, Pam and Dodd, Philip (eds) *Women and Film: A 'Sight and Sound' Reader*, London: Scarlet Press, 123–32.

Taubin, Amy (2000) 'The allure of decay' in Arroyo, José (ed.) *Action/Spectacle Cinema*, London: British Film Institute, 150–55.

Zigno, Federico de (1998) *Cittadini X: Serial Killer dalla realtà allo schermo*, Florence: Tarab.

11

FOUR FILMS OF
LANA TURNER

Despite the enormous interest in stars, there has been very little study of them, and this has predominantly been sociological, concerned with how stars function in general ideological/cultural terms. Such concerns are certainly central to film studies, but we also need to know how stars function within the films themselves, that is, how the films articulate, carry, inflect, or subvert the general ideological/cultural functions. This article examines the way a single star image, Lana Turner's, is variously used in films in relation to other elements such as the construction of character, narrative, *mise-en-scène* and so on.[1]

Why Lana Turner? In part, certainly, because I like her; but her work also illustrates certain characteristic features of the star phenomenon. The four films discussed use her in different ways. In *Ziegfeld Girl*, the Turner image sends the film off-course and in effect partly cracks open its central mythology, whereas in *The Postman Always Rings Twice* (hereinafter, *Postman*) the image both holds together and exposes contradictory elements. *The Bad and the Beautiful* elaborates upon and finally celebrates the image, while *Imitation of Life* examines and scrutinizes it, holding it up to the light to expose it. More generally, Turner illustrates three of the ways that stars function *cinematically* (that is, within the total signifying practice of the cinema industry situated within society as a whole).

1 Her career is marked by an unusually, even spectacularly, high degree of interpenetration between her publicly available private life and her films. The star phenomenon depends upon collapsing the distinction between the star-as-person and the star-as-performer. This does not usually mean that the incidents of a film's scenario are taken to be actual incidents in the star's life but rather that they reveal or express the personality or type-of-person of the star. In the case of Turner, however, not only do her vehicles furnish characters and situations in accord with her off-screen image, but frequently incidents in them echo incidents in her life so that by the end of her career films like *Peyton Place, Imitation*

79

of Life, Madame X and *Love Has Many Faces* seem in parts like mere illustrations of her life.

2   In the earlier films, Turner's image exemplifies one of the major forms of relationship between a star and her/his social context, namely the reconciliation of contradictions. Stars frequently speak to dominant contradictions in social life – experienced as conflicting demands, contrary expectations, irreconcilable but equally held values – in such a way as to appear to reconcile them. In part, by simply being one indivisible entity with an existence in the 'real world', yet displaying contradictory personality traits, stars can affirm that it is possible to triumph over, transcend, successfully live out contradictions. In the case of Turner, this centres on her being strongly sexual, both for herself and for others (therefore in Hollywood-American terms, extraordinary) but also ordinary. As Jeanine Basinger puts it, 'She was as much the ice cream parlor as she was the perfumed boudoir' (1976: 11). An interesting feature of Turner's career is that films and publicity seem continually to be condemning or punishing her for this daring combination, yet her survival and growth as an identification figure bespeak the hold of such a magic reconciliation of opposites on the cinematic imagination.

3   In Turner's later films, the processes of manufacture – the production of the image – are increasingly evident until they become an integral part of the image. With most stars, the point is to disguise the manufacturing so that they simply appear to be what their image proclaims them to be; with Turner, part of the fascination is with the manufacture itself – with her, it is actually beguiling to see the strings being pulled. This is especially true of *The Bad and the Beautiful* and *Imitation of Life*, and also of the Joe Morella and Edward Z. Epstein biography *Lana* (1972) which focuses as much on the fabrication of Lana as on the 'reality' of Judy Turner.

Ziegfeld Girl (1941)

Ziegfeld Girl inherits from Turner's previous career her sexy-ordinary image. In the process of building on it, however, the film gets severely out of joint, turning a production-values-laden musical into quite a serious drama. The Turner parts of the film make explicit what also comes across in the Judy Garland and Hedy Lamarr parts – a fumbling, confused critique of the notion of woman as spectacle at its most glorified, to wit, the Ziegfeld girl.

The sexy-ordinary configuration of the Turner image was crystallized in four moments in her career prior to *Ziegfeld Girl*: her first film role in *They Won't Forget* (1937), her sweater-girl pin-ups, her marriage to Artie Shaw and her starlet roles taken as a whole.

In *They Won't Forget*, she plays a young woman whose every action breathes sexuality – getting her male schoolteacher all flustered, telling a soda-jerk to put an egg in her malted milk 'as fresh as you', and walking down the street with hips swaying and breasts bouncing. She is raped and murdered. The ordinary setting and the ordinary clothes, together with the extraordinary appeal, would be enough to inflame any real man, the film seems to imply (and we never get to know who the rapist and murderer in fact is), and in so far as the film was a message film, it was a protest against the corruption of the South rather than against rape.

The sweater-girl pin-ups (Figure 11.1) date from Turner's appearance in *They Won't Forget*, but they became so widespread in the subsequent build-up that their meaning became rather more generalized. They encapsulate the sexy-ordinary configuration. On the one hand, a sweater is not a glamour garment – it is something cheap, practical, available everywhere. (In none of the portraits does Turner appear to be wearing an extravagantly styled sweater or one made of costly stuff.) On the other hand, worn by Turner, it became blatantly erotic, showing off the breasts, clinging to the waist. The rigid separation of women stars into homely-but-sexless (loose or flattening garments, including sweaters) or sexy-but-exotic (fetishistic fabrics, outlandish designs heightening body features) was collapsed. The girl-next-door was that never-never sex bombshell, plain-knit and voyeur's delight were one.

In February 1940, Turner eloped with Artie Shaw. Four months later, she divorced him. Although sex in a direct form was not mentioned in the coverage of these events, they are still an inflection of the sexy-ordinary configuration. Shaw was a band leader, and the bands were the courtship, dating, heterosexual romance music of the day. Turner's first marriage was at the heart of America's love-and-sex culture. It was also impulsive, although this was not necessarily viewed as a negative quality – it could be considered charmingly youthful, though it had already intimations of immaturity. More important, it was over in four months. Turner's publicly available life was going wrong; something was going sour in the heart of ordinariness.

Certain patterns of the Turner image, then, were beginning to take shape – sexiness perceived in ordinariness, but also associations of this with youth/immaturity and trouble. The starlet roles between *They Won't Forget* and *Ziegfeld Girl* do not appear to have elaborated upon this, but it is clear that the ambiguity of Turner's image was sufficient for MGM to feel equally happy casting her as a good girl (*We Who Are Young*, 1940) or a bad (*Love Finds Andy Hardy*, 1938), a sexpot (*Calling Dr Kildare*, 1939) or a down-to-earth student (*Dramatic School*, 1938). A star's physiognomy carries the meanings of her/his image in whatever film she or he makes, in whatever character she or he plays (cf. Alloway 1972). Thus, short of being strenuously performed against the image, it is likely that by 1940 the character played by Turner, just because it was played by her, was already sexy-ordinary, no matter whether the film made something of it or not and virtually regardless of the character as scripted.

81

Figure 11.1 The sweater girl

Ziegfeld Girl is very conscious of the images of its three main stars, Turner, Garland and Lamarr. Narrative and treatment are tailored to them. Garland is established as having a vaudeville background and thus all the know-how of the born-in-a-trunk pro; she is dressed in little-girl suits and has her requisite wistful follow-up to 'Over the Rainbow' in 'I'm Always Chasing Rainbows' as well as her jazzy, up-tempo spot, 'Minnie from Trinidad'. With Lamarr, everything promotes her remote, exotic beauty – she is foreign, married to a violinist (hence associated with Artistic Beauty), and has no thought of becoming a Ziegfeld girl when the star of the show (Frank Merton/Tony Martin) is stunned by her beauty as he passes her; a glistening close-up shot of her is often inserted into her scenes with other people (whereas it never is of Turner or Garland), which effectively sets her apart from the interaction; in the numbers, she is the statuesque central figure, coming closest to Ziegfeld's prescriptions for his 'girls'. The film's overall structure can accommodate these two images – they can be used effectively in the numbers, and fit two show-business women types (though, as I'll argue below, there are elements of criticism of Ziegfeld girlhood even in Lamarr and Garland). Turner (Sheila) fits less happily.

The film begins by building on the ordinary side of the Turner configuration. She is 'discovered' operating a lift in a department store. Neither a pro nor an exotic beauty, she is just an ordinary working girl rocketed to stardom. This conforms with the publicity surrounding Turner's own discovery at a soda fountain in a Hollywood Boulevard drug-store (this is inaccurate, though not drastically so), and meteoric rise to fame (it took rather longer than was publicly known). Her first act on being asked to audition for Ziegfeld is to go and try on an exorbitantly priced leopard-skin coat. This again conforms with her image as a girl who gets a real lift out of possessions. As one fan magazine of the period noted,

> She glitters whether on the beach, in the drawing room, or in the studio restaurant dressed in gingham. She admits she enjoys the luxury that stardom has brought her. And she drives a fire-engine red coupé. Lana is the most spectacular personality to be thrown up by films since Clara Bow.

Thus far, *Ziegfeld Girl* is simply reproducing a facet of Turner's image. However, as both Basinger and Morella/Epstein state, during the making of the film, MGM and the director, Robert Z. Leonard, were so impressed by Turner that they expanded her role. This affects the film in three ways – building on the elements of the Turner image adds complexity to that image, the impact of her role comes into conflict with the musical's generic requirements, and her increasing centrality also calls into question the film's central motif.

Building on the image of the ordinary girl rocketed to a fame she luxuriates in brings in the complexity of response claimed by the Turner sexy-ordinary image. There is certainly a basic level of delight of the kind the fan magazine evinced. But there is also and equally pathos and condemnation. The impulsive desire to spend, and spend big, is perhaps in itself sympathetic, and is rendered more so in a key scene between Sheila/Turner and her old truck-driver boyfriend Gil (James Stewart). Her desire is located in deprivation, a deprivation the film is careful to link not with her class situation but with her unlucky experience as a child of always being the one who arrived at a party 'after the ice cream ran out'. We are asked to be sorry for her – doubly so when, running after Gil as he leaves in disgust, she trips on the minks she has strewn before him to proclaim her new wealth. We are here being asked to be sorry for her materialism, for what led to it in the first place and what it is doing to her now. Yet in her pursuit of wealth, she goes to the bad. She acquires a sugar daddy, Geoffrey, then, when he snubs her, she takes to drink, is suspended from the Follies and winds up in a seedy bar with Jimmy, also a down-and-out. It is no longer clear what sort of response is being elicited. She has broken taboos on women's behaviour – losing her man by demanding he adapt to her life-style, getting drunk. These demand condemnation by the conventions of the film's day, and I do not know how far the pathos elements let her off the hook. This ambiguity, the 'bad' woman who suffers for her badness and thus becomes an identification/sympathy figure, is the emotional timbre that is caught in all her subsequent films.

As the dramatic-pathetic elements increase with Sheila/Turner's downfall, so they come to occupy the centre of the film. Not only does this mean that the other two star characters' careers are given short shrift (as narrative developments in musicals often are), but it also begins to interfere with what is a musical's *raison d'être*, the numbers. Throughout it is clear that the numbers do not quite know what to do with Turner – she has no musical gifts (or none that film has ever developed), and although she would be fine as one of the chorines in Busby Berkeley's Warners Depression musicals, the kind of thing Berkeley is staging here, all haughty parading and baroque headdresses and trains, does not suit her small frame and 'common' face – not yet in her career anyway. By the time of the last big production number, 'You Gotta Pull Strings', the Sheila/Turner plot dominates everything and, since the point is that she is not in this number, having been suspended from the Follies, the emotional weight in the cross-cutting between the number and her in the theatre watching is decidedly with her. All the more so when, unable to watch any more, despite having struggled out of her alcohol-induced sick-bed to be there, she leaves the auditorium and the film stays with her and not the number. As she hears the final walk-down music strike up on stage, she holds herself up and begins to walk down the entrance stairs. Thus for the climax of the number (and of all the numbers in the film) we see Turner in the 'surrounding' narrative and not the girls in the 'central' number.

This final walk-down also has a further significance in the film. The walk-down is the defining motif of the Ziegfeld show – it is the moment at which the girls parade themselves and are thus 'glorified'. It is used five times in relation to Sheila/Turner. The first is in the first big production number, 'You Stepped out of a Dream' (Figure 11.2). In this, the camera follows Turner as she walks down the circling ramp. Garland and Lamarr are not similarly treated, although the latter is given a couple of cut-in close-ups of her sculptured face, and she is distinguished from both Garland and Turner by her dress, which is more *haute couture*, less show-girl in style. The effect of the camera sticking with Turner in this number, which for all three characters is their first night as Ziegfeld girls, is to stress her excitement at being a Ziegfeld girl and to associate the walk-down especially with her. The second use of the walk-down motif takes place the next morning at Turner's home (she is still living with her parents): she is trudging down the stairs until her brother says 'Here comes the glamour girl!' – then she straightens up, and descends the stairs as if on stage for the walk-down (Figure 11.3). Again, in the night-club in Florida, she walks down some stairs as if she and they are in the Follies, only this time it is after quarrelling with Gil and drinking too much champagne. Each walk-down is registering a moment in her career. The next is on stage in the 'Minnie from Trinidad' number, during which she collapses, drunk, and the last is during 'You Gotta Pull Strings', as described above.

The walk-down motif in relation to Sheila/Turner links her decline – which the film, as we've seen, also explains in terms of deprivation, materialism and going to the bad – to the core of the Zeigfeld show. In this way, by association, the whole enterprise of Ziegfeld – his girls, woman as spectacle

84

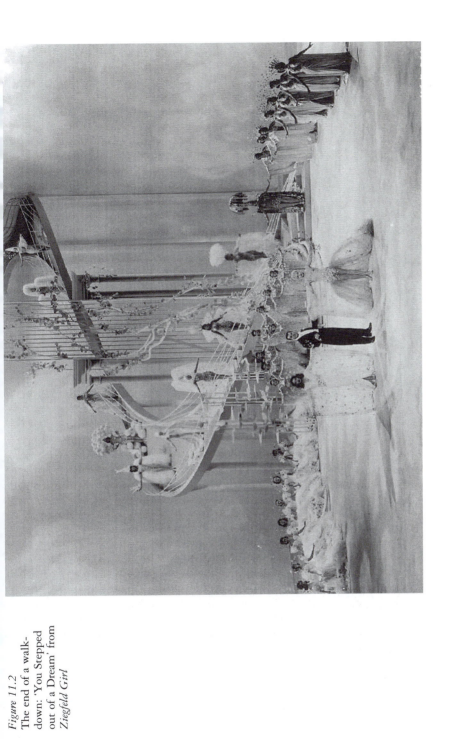

Figure 11.2
The end of a walk-
down: 'You Stepped
out of a Dream' from
Ziegfeld Girl

Figure 11.3
The end of a walk-
down at home in
Ziegfeld Girl

– which the film was clearly set up to celebrate, is called into question. There are intimations of this through the Garland and Lamarr characters. The only one of the three to make it to the top is Garland – but then she has her roots in vaudeville, which is signalled in the film, through the character of her father, as being a more vital and authentic entertainment tradition. (Her father is played by Charles Winniger; in the film he teams up with Al Shean in a re-creation of Gallagher and Shean, one of the legendary acts on the vaudeville circuit; this happens just before the enfeebled 'You Gotta Pull Strings' number and 'brings the house down'; effectively, vaudeville has the last say in the film's numbers.) Lamarr, on the other hand, leaves the Follies to join her husband when he gets a job; the very haughty beauty which makes her an epitome of the Ziegfeld girl also makes her 'superior' to show business. Between Garland and Lamarr, Ziegfeld gets it from low and high-brows.

What Sheila/Turner adds to this is sex. Clearly, despite the 'Glorifying the American girl' tag, Ziegfeld was peddling sexuality – but the glorifica-tion idea, his use of famous couturiers and chic designers, appeared to elevate his shows above the despised burlesque (which means striptease in American usage). Sheila/Turner drags it down again. Partly, the film takes on Turner's association with sexuality just by having her in it. In addition, some of the dialogue draws attention to the Ziegfeld project, as when Patsy (Eve Arden) wisecracks to the girls about their make-up, 'Don't worry dear, they won't be looking at your face.' It is on Sheila/Turner's legs that the camera dwells in this first walk-down, aided by the wide parting in her sequined dress. And, again unlike Garland or Lamarr, it is as a pin-up that she acquires off-stage fame, even winding up on the wall of the garage where Gil works. The crystallization of all this round Sheila/Turner and her special association with the walk-down motif puts a dent in the hypocrisy of Ziegfeld's glittering sex show. Add to that the emotional weighting given her, her virtually eclipsing the numbers by the end, and one can see how the decision to build on Turner's star image leads the film almost to overturn its own project. The brief scene of reconciliation with Gil (they are going to go to the country to breed ducks) and a perfunctory shot of Garland atop a wedding-cake-style set hardly suffice to set the film properly back on course.

The Postman Always Rings Twice (1946)

Between *Ziegfeld Girl* and *Postman*, Turner's sexy-ordinary image was consol-idated. The war proved useful for this. Nothing is more ordinary in the public imagination than the serviceman. Thus the fact that, for instance, the sailors of the SS *Idaho* voted her their favourite star, that she married a serviceman in life (Stephen Crane) and in a film (*Marriage Is a Private Affair*, 1944), and herself joined the WACS in *Keep Your Powder Dry* (1945), all preserved her association with ordinariness. Equally, they preserved the association of that with other things – with plain sexiness in the case of the SS *Idaho* men – and throughout the war Turner was a major pin-up in men' magazines. The marriage to Crane (1942) went wrong – she married on impulse again, as with Shaw, knowing next to nothing about him; he was however, already married, so the marriage had to be annulled; then he got a divorce, but she would not remarry him and he tried to commit suicide twice; she discovered she was pregnant and they remarried; a year later (1944) they divorced, with Turner getting custody of the baby, Cheryl Following the Shaw fiasco, it was as if Turner and marriage (ordinary marriage to ordinary men) did not go. Not that Shaw or Crane came out of it well but both marriages set off the central Turner ambiguity – what she touches turns bad, but is that because she is bad or because she is irresistibly attracted to the bad? (And is being attracted to the bad itself badness?) *Marriage Is a Private Affair* similarly dealt with a GI's marriage (after a three-day courtship going off the rails, through his wife's (Turner's) infidelity, though all ends happily. More generally, Turner's status as sexy leading lady was confirmed by her teamings with Clark Gable in *Honky Tonk* (1941) and *Somewhere I'l Find You* (1942).

These ambiguities, the role of impulse, the play on badness and on the sexy-ordinary configuration, all came in useful for the Turner character, Cora in *Postman*. Without them, the film courts incoherence in its construction of this central character.

I want to consider *Postman* chiefly in terms of the key but neglected question of how a character is constructed in a film. What I want to suggest is that there are here three different methods of character construction, which fit uneasily together. These methods are structural (we understand characters by what they do in the plot or how they function in the narrative) motivational (the reasons provided by dialogue and sometimes other elements such as performance and *mise-en-scène* as to why a character does such-and such a thing) and star-based (the star's image already gives the character a certain set of traits). These methods contribute to the construction of an apparently autonomous character (rather than one acknowledged as an aspect of the film's point(s)-of-view) – corresponding, of course, to how we normally talk about characters, ascribing motives and feelings to them as if they are real people independent of us and a narrative's author.

The initial problem with *Postman* is who the film is really about Structurally, it is a *film noir*, which means that, like nearly all *films noirs*, the narrative is centred on the male protagonist (Frank/John Garfield). His voice over leads into the film and recurs at various points until we realize he has been telling his story to a priest in prison. Since the film ends there and the priest has been the listener, a certain status is conferred retrospectively on Frank as both the subject of the narrative and its truthful narrator. The film can then be seen as being 'about' the hero's doom. The sense of doom, fate entrapment is reinforced by the obsessive doubling of events and images in the film, both major narrative incidents (two accidents with a lorry, two attempts to kill the husband Nick, two attempts to leave the café, two trials for murder) and minor details of treatment (two lipstick rolls, two vital notes left in the cash register, two pushes at the car on the second attempt on Nick's life, the echoes at the lake, the name of the café, The Twin Oaks, and the title of the film).

In this context, the woman is a function of the ensnaring structure. The *femme fatale* need not necessarily be evil, but she is the means by which the hero gets drawn into the plot, and hence his doom. Indeed, it is more to the point if she is not simply and utterly evil, for it is precisely the hero's uncertainty on this point, the very unknowability of Woman, that really traps him. (Much of the pleasure of *film noir* resides in the true knowledge of the woman, as good or evil, vouchsafed the hero and hence the (male?) audience at the end; e.g. *The Maltese Falcon, The Lady from Shanghai, Chinatown*.)

At one level, Cora in *Postman* is a mere function of the film's structure. She is only there to be the means by which Frank enters the path that leads to his doom, to be the terrible object of his sexuality, terrible because his attraction to her is what leads him to the death cell. Her famous first appearance – the roll of her lipstick along the floor attracting his (and the camera's) attention, followed by a track back along the floor, up her bare legs to her white shorts and halter top – is very directly sexual, and throughout the film her brilliant white clothes are both eye-catching and a sign of the heat of the summer (with all that connotes). The wretchedness of women, in the mind of *film noir*, is that they are such a turn-on for the hero, with disastrous consequences for him (compare the logic of *They Won't Forget*). One can see Cora functioning like this throughout the film's structure.

Yet even in the first scene, it is not as simple as that. On the one hand, Cora as herself a subject is implied – the 'Man Wanted' sign in the opening shots of the film hangs over the scene, we can assume she has rolled the lipstick herself, and the manner in which she does her lips while looking at him suggests a deliberate making of herself into an object of desire. On the other hand, the burning hamburger, so obviously a symbol of lighted passions, and the general atmosphere of heat suggest a sexual force generated between them both (a sense referred to by almost every reviewer as 'the chemistry' 'sparked' between Garfield and Turner). A sense of Cora as herself a force acting on the narrative derives from the motivational level of character construction in *Postman* being as emphatic as the structural. Cora, and Cora-and-Frank, are provided with reasons for doing things, whereas in other *films noirs* only Frank would be.

Yet as soon as this motivational level comes into play, further problems arise. If one looks at the motives Cora is provided with, they are ambiguous and contradictory almost to the point of incoherence. Why, as indicated by the film, does Cora get Frank to kill Nick? Because, pitiably, she is trapped into a marriage with a dreary older man, largely because she was fed up with

89

other men bothering her ('I was never homey . . . I never met a man since I was fifteen who didn't want to give me an argument about it'). And because she is ambitious (her repeated statements to the effect that she wants 'to make something' of herself and the café). And because she loves Frank (she leaves the café with him; her direct, i.e. 'genuine', outburst in the kitchen after she has been contemplating suicide with a kitchen knife, 'If you really love me, you would . . .'), and/or is manipulating him (in an earlier kitchen scene, we get a close-up on 'Can't you see how happy we'd be together?' in which her shifting eyes clearly signal manipulation). And because she is driven by a bad sexuality (the scenes on the beach; her provocative clothes; images of heat). Partly, what is happening here is that the film wants to give Cora motivations, including some that make her a sympathetic figure, but, as her (generic) function in the narrative is to be changeable and unknowable, the film has to keep giving her different, inconsistent motivations. Yet inconsistency on this scale risks being simply incoherent. The film's devices would betray themselves all too quickly without Lana Turner in the part.

Because it is Turner, the contradictions of Cora, and Cora-and-Frank, get an emphasis which amounts to a resolution (more or less – perceptions will differ on this). Cora is sexy-ordinary: her speech about not being 'homey' indicates this clearly enough, as indeed does the extraordinary sexual charge she carries in so suffocatingly dull a setting. The various motivations she is provided with can be loosely organized around the badness syndrome developed in Turner's image. She is attracted to the bad (adultery, murder); this makes her pitiable (she is trapped both by her situation of marriage and by the inexorable repetitions of the plot once she strays from marriage), but it also intimates that she may herself be bad (her sexuality, her manipulation and prompting of Frank to murder). Notions of coherence of character do not permit the coexistence of such traits (except under the rubric of woman the capricious and unknowable, which is not allowable here since, on the contrary, we know too much, and of that much is sympathetic), but notions of the star reconciling or holding in tension key contradictions in the culture (and thus effectively transcending them) do permit them to a certain extent. However, in the process, certain traits are subordinated. Thus Cora's driving ambition, which is granted legitimacy at the motivational level simply in terms of the time allowed it and the straight treatment of it, lacks force since it has no place in the Turner complex. As a result, one either ignores the ambition motive, or denies it legitimacy by regarding it as falsehood or manipulation, or merely feels that it does not fit.

The motivations of Cora-and-Frank, as a couple and as murderers, are also aided by Turner's presence, though here she is less crucial to the film's coherence. The key to their murderous relationship is impulse. In each of the scenes in which they contemplate murder, a crash of music, where before there was none, signals the thought of murder arising from nowhere rational in their minds. The first of these scenes occurs after Nick, returning drunk from the laundry, nearly crashes into a lorry. Frank blurts out, 'I'd like to see him get plastered like that and drive off a cliff'; music in; they look at each other as Cora says, 'You didn't mean that, you were joking', and Frank replies, ''Course I was'; they kiss. The idea for murder arises spontaneously; music signals its impact; a kiss links it to passion. (In an earlier scene, Frank's suggestion of Cora wanting to make money so as to have some set aside when her husband dies is also met by music and a kiss, though murder as such is not mentioned.) The second such scene takes place in Frank's bedroom. Having elicited from him that he loves her, Cora, fingering the lapel of the dressing-gown he is wearing, says, 'There's one thing we could do.' Frank replies, 'Pray for something to happen to Nick,' and Cora says, 'Something like that'; music in; Frank exclaims, 'Cora!' Here the link between passion and murder is clearer, but murder is not actually directly referred to. It is clearly in Cora's mind, but she does not have to say the word for Frank to latch on. The music signals its arousal in their 'chemistry'. The third scene takes place in the kitchen, after Frank has discovered Cora with a kitchen knife in her hand. Here there is a more directly expressed impulsive outburst from Cora – 'If you really love me, you would . . .'; pause; Frank, 'All right'; music in; Cora, 'No!' This last exclamation suggests that the idea for murder arose in her head without premeditation. Once again, the music suggests the intention to murder is an impulse rather than a rational or cold-blooded plan.

The film, then, does a lot of work on the notion of impulse, even without the input of Turner as Cora. The particular inflection she adds is suffering from one's own impulses. Her impulsive marriages in life had led to suffering of one kind and another, and the film roles reprised this. Consequently the pattern of impulse and entrapment in *Postman* can be read – I would argue, *was* read by Turner's fans – as a source of identification and sympathy. The attraction to bad (often meaning little more than sexual desire) can be seen as an uncontrollable, destroying impulse that anyone can identify with (especially in a sex-negative culture). Yet this means that, at the level of the star image's contribution to character, the film is about Cora at least as much as it is about Frank, even though structurally she is a mere function of his destiny. Thus, if in terms of the relationship between the motivational and star image levels, Turner serves to mask the contradictions of the *femme fatale* type (a type of course that reflects the male construction – and fear – of the female), in terms of the relationship between the structural and star levels, Turner serves to open up the tension between what women are for men and what that means for women as women. (I am not positing here either any brilliance on Turner's part – though I would never wish to denigrate her performing abilities – nor an untutored feminist sensibility on the part of director, writer, or whoever; it is rather that in the relationship between her life/films and women audiences, a certain registering and defining of the female experience in this society was possible and that this happens in *Postman* simply because she is in it.) If that accounts for the film's near-incoherence and unsatisfactory feel, it also accounts for the fascination of its elusive play of fate and motivation.

The Bad and the Beautiful (1953)

In both *Ziegfeld Girl* and *Postman*, Turner's image contributes to the overall meaning of the film, partially undermining it in the former, largely coming to its rescue in the latter. With *The Bad and the Beautiful* (1953) and *Imitation of Life* (1959), the image itself becomes in part the subject-matter of the film. By this time, however, the image's meaning has shifted in certain respects. The sexy-ordinary configuration has become 'glamour' (or, 'Lanallure'), and the badness both more extreme and more pitiable. Both these developments are reproduced, and celebrated, in *The Bad and the Beautiful*.

Glamour and ordinariness are antithetical notions. The ordinary and the everyday are by definition not glamorous. Yet glamour – or the particular inflection of the notion embodied by Turner – is based on manufacture, and can be seen to be the process, the industrial process, by which the ordinary is rendered the glamorous. The glamour industry, in which Hollywood played a decisive part, sold itself on the idea that, given its products, anyone – any woman, anyway – could become beautiful. Turner was living proof of this, and if, later in her career, none of the original material – the ordinary woman – showed through any more, this was all the more proof that the glamour process worked.

Turner's career as a pin-up illustrates this transition and also helps to identify the notion of glamour. The early examples make reference to the social world as a whole, outside of Hollywood. In Figure 11.4, taken when she was 17 (1938), this is done by a certain 'naturalism'. Artful as the photo actually is, it is meant to look spontaneous, just catching the girl on a turn, and we are not supposed to notice the elements of lighting, retouching, etc. The loosely coiffed hair, the type of expression, the apparent absence of make-up, all impose a notion of a natural, ordinary girl. Figure 11.5, on the other hand, is very obviously a studio photograph (taken in 1940) with its 'odd' angle, arch pose and obvious set. Yet despite that, it is still full of social referents – the 'bad girl' expression, the tousled (= sexually loose) hair, the dress with its busy jungle print. The social reference of the sweater-girl pin-ups has already been discussed. Thus, for all their artifice, whether or not obvious, these photographs do relate Turner to social types, attitudes, values and life-styles in the 'everyday world'. (The everyday world is of course fiction – it is not the world that we actually experience every day, but rather the world that we assume is *typically* experienced by other people. Needless to add, much of the definition of what constitutes the typically everyday derives from the mass media.) The later examples, on the other hand, refer to a self-enclosed, self-defined world of glamour. The images are static, the compositional values less dynamic (compare the half-turn of the head and holding of the pearls in Figure 11.6 with the sharp round-over-the-shoulder look of Figures 11.4 and 11.5, or compare the essentially circular pattern made by the later examples, the arms serving to bring the eye back to the body, with the sweater-girl pose of Figure 11.1 – the arms thrust away from the body and the thrusting breasts and knees). These later pin-ups (they date from 1958–60) inhabit a glazed, plastic, perfectly 'finished' world. Any movement would disturb the lighting, as it catches the hair in Figure 11.6, moulds the face in Figure 11.7 and creates patterns in Figure 11.8. And the only reference outside this world is to the world of glamorous consumption – expensive possessions such as pearls, furs, evening dresses and expensive services of hairdressing and cosmetics. This self-enclosed world of glamour, glorying in its own artifice, is brought into sharper focus by the press photograph (taken in 1951) of Turner with her friend Ava Gardner (Figure 11.9). Gardner represents a notion of natural, 'animal' beauty. Although this is as manufactured as any other image of beauty, the manufacture is less obvious – her hair is loosely dressed, she wears a plain blouse and simple pearls, her expression is direct. Turner on the other hand bespeaks manufacture in every detail, down to the slightly held-off pose against Gardner.

It is this element of manufactured glamour that is emphasized in *The Bad and the Beautiful*. Whenever there is a break in the filming within the film, a hairdresser or make-up artist steps in to retouch Georgia/Turner's look (they are in fact played by Turner's personal hairdresser, Helen Young, and make-up man, Del Armstrong). The screen-test sequence opens with a close-up of her eyebrow being painted in – as any assiduous reader of the fan magazines would have known, Turner had had her eyebrows shaved off for the role of an oriental handmaiden during the filming of *The Adventures of Marco Polo* in 1938, and they never grew again. This shot is (like the casting of hairdresser and make-up man) part in-joke, but also part reinforcement of the idea of the manufacture of glamour, not just by heightening beauty that is already there but also by creating artificial beauty where there is nothing.

By emphasizing manufacture, the film also emphasizes the star image as an illusion. This is evoked in the first shot of Georgia/Turner. A maid answers the phone and says it is Mr Shields; the camera moves across (is it to another room, or was the maid a reflection in a mirror?), showing us in quick succession first Georgia side-on in a mirror, then her back, then her face full-on in a mirror. Already the film is giddy with reflection images, reflections, moreover, of a woman preparing her appearance at a dressing-table. How can we, as we watch, pick out the levels of illusion here? – the illusion of reflection, the illusion of make-up, the illusion of the film we are watching . . . Georgia/Turner puts a black lace veil over her head, then turns to listen at the telephone receiver. The camera now finally homes in on her face (rather than the reflection of it), stopping at a perfectly composed glamour framing.

Figure 11.4 Early pin-up of Lana Turner I

Figure 11.4 Early pin-up of Lana Turner II

Figure 11.6 Later pin-up of Lana Turner I

Figure 11.7 Later pin-up of Lana Turner II

Figure 11.8 Later pin-up of Lana Turner III

Figure 11.9 Lana Turner and Ava Gardner in greeting

The final frame of this brief one-take, then, is both really Georgia (or Turner . . .), not her reflection, and yet is also she at her most 'produced'.

What we have got in the final frame is the *real illusion*. For it is no part of the purpose of *The Bad and the Beautiful* to demystify glamour by fore-grounding its manufacture. Rather, the processes of manufacture themselves become fascinating and . . . glamorous. The same holds true for the film's overall depiction of Hollywood. It is rather like a conjuror showing you how a trick is done by quickness of the hand – you are so impressed by the dexterity that you remain as dazzled by how the trick is done as you were before by its magic effect. (This relates to Minnelli's other films; cf. Cook 1977.)

Nor is this emphasis on the glamour of illusion-manufacture meant to detract from the notion of the star's special quality or magic. On the contrary it is the techniques of illusion that stimulate the 'real magic' of the star, the 'truth' of her 'performance'. (The oxymoronic brilliance of *The Bad and the Beautiful* will finally defeat me.) In the dialogue, we have repeated insistences that Georgia is a star. This has nothing to do with talent or acting ability, but, as Jonathan (Kirk Douglas) says after her screen-test, the fact that, no matter how bad she may be, no one can take their eyes off her when she is on the screen. Similarly, Jonathan dismisses Lucien's objection that Georgia does not have the poise for a period costume the former has designed observing that Georgia is a star and will therefore be all right. She need only to be tutored to bring out this innate quality. In the processing of the raw material, the hidden value – star quality – will be revealed. (The film apparently wants to insist that this is not a question of conning the public – nowhere in *The Bad and the Beautiful* is the apparatus of fan magazines, promotion and so on shown directly to have a role in star manufacture although the press agent, Syd, is seen as a permanent member of the creative studio team.)

In the working-out of the narrative, this play on reality and illusion comes to a mesmerizing climax. Jonathan cannot get the right effect from Georgia in the marriage scene in the film they are shooting. When they pack up for the day, they have a quiet exchange during which Georgia gazes longingly at him. 'That's the expression I want!' he says. As a result, Georgia pours her feeling for him into the role in the film. It is this that gives 'truth' to her performance. Yet the film has hinted, and is soon to reveal, that he is merely manipulating her. In other words, the truth of her performance rests on a deception.

When Georgia herself realizes this, discovering him at home with another woman during the première party, we have the famous car scene, in which in one long take, she drives into the night, crying hysterically, with head lights glaring into her (and our) eyes, the rain lashing down, the camera twisting around her. What we seem to be getting here is the moment of real reality, assured by the notion that only untrammelled, chaotic, violent emotion is authentic. All the rest is illusion. It is the supreme masterstroke to fabricate this authenticity so completely in a studio mock-up of a car and with the epitome of star artifice, Lana Turner.

Turner's association with badness continued as a defining element of her publicly available private life between *Postman* and *The Bad and the Beautiful*. She dated countless men, most of them famous, and hence was widely rumoured to be a nymphomaniac (or, as an MGM executive quoted by Morella and Epstein revealingly put it, 'Lana had the morals and the attitudes of a man. . . . If she saw a muscular stage hand with tight pants and she liked him, she'd invite him into her dressing-room'). In 1947, she married Bob Topping, a wealthy heir, three days after his divorce from a previous marriage (in which she was named as co-respondent). The Presbyterian minister who married them was, with much publicity directed against Turner, suspended because Presbyterians are not allowed to marry people divorced for less than a year. In 1951, she was separated from Topping; she had an accident in her shower, variously put down to drunkenness, suicide attempt, or pure accident. The films of the period, however – apart from her role as the thoroughly wicked Lady de Winter in *The Three Musketeers* (1948) – do not reflect this emphasis on badness. What does characterize them, apart from their use of Turner as a glamour object, is a tendency to team her with considerably older men, including Spencer Tracy in *Cass Timberlaine* (1947) and a visibly ageing Clark Gable in *Homecoming* (1948; this was their third film together, but the difference in their ages was more apparent than before).

This teaming is of a piece with the emergence in Turner's publicity, as crucially related to her association with badness, of the role of her father. Early in her career, MGM had invented a biography for Turner, giving her a wealthy father ('a mining engineer') who had died in an accident. In fact, she came from a very poor home; her father, who had once been a miner, was a gambler and bootlegger and was murdered by one of his cronies when Turner was ten. The studio had wanted to fabricate Turner as an All American Girl – but when her image was clearly anything but harmed by her turning to the bad, it became useful to let the true story of Turner's past be known via fan magazines, biographies, etc. The inexorable link with badness, and its pitiability, was strengthened by the image of both her sordid origins and her loss of her father. This got her all ways: she was indelibly bad, but could not help it, genetically (who her father was), environmentally (the upbringing he gave her) and psychologically (loss of him at a crucial age made the passage to mature heterosexuality problematic). In a culture as drenched, even at the popular level, in naturalizing, individuated explanations of personality as America in the 1940s and 1950s, Turner and her father were a powerful image-complex. In an interview, Turner herself suggested the meaning of her father's death – 'Since my life has been wayward and impulsive, always a search for something that is not there, and then disillusionment, I believe I need all the excuses I can make. The shock I suffered then may be a valid excuse for me now. It may explain things I do not myself understand' (quoted by Morella and Epstein).

The idea that Turner's relations with men are somehow related to the early death of her father gives a certain *frisson* to many of her roles – for example, Sheila has a sugar daddy in *Ziegfeld Girl*, Nick in *Postman* is old enough to be Cora's father. But this is all very oblique. With *The Bad and the Beautiful*, it is the key to the relationship between Georgia and Jonathan. What follows is not a psychoanalytic reading of *The Bad and the Beautiful*, much less of Georgia and Jonathan; it is rather an analysis of a text that is, rather obviously, informed by popular psychoanalysis, as indeed many films directed by Vincente Minnelli are. Their fathers bring them together; her dependence upon him depends upon her rejecting her real father and replacing him with Jonathan; the question is whether she can in turn reject this surrogate father.

Their fathers bring them together, although both are dead. Georgia's father, an actor, worked for Jonathan's, a producer, just as Georgia and Jonathan are actor and producer respectively. Georgia's father drew a picture of Jonathan's father, as a demon with a pitchfork, on the (?nursery) wall of his home. It is here that Jonathan and Georgia (legs only visible, dangling from a loft) first meet. Jonathan removes the drawing from the wall, and hangs it in his office. When she goes, an unknown bit player, for an audition there, it is her turning to look at the drawing (together with her lustrous blonde hair seen earlier when she is working as a stand-in) that identifies her to Jonathan. It is moreover her turning, with an identical movement of the head, to look at the drawing in studio boss Harry Pebbel's office in the film's framing story that leads into her flashback of her relationship with Jonathan. This relationship is thus signalled at various important moments by her father's hostile feelings towards his father.

He 'kills' her father. She has 'built a shrine to him' (Jonathan's words) and he breaks it up, smashing the record of her father intoning a *Macbeth* soliloquy, drawing a moustache on a picture of him. As a result, she is free of her father – but by substituting Jonathan. In the scene after he has dropped her in the pool (she has gone out and got drunk through fear on the night before shooting begins), Geogia/Turner performs just like a little girl. The accoutrements of glamour are replaced by a head towel and outsize coat (it is his, but it makes her look like the archetypal little girl wearing a grown-up's clothes). She sits first on the floor, then on his knee – never in an equal adult position. She speaks, in a little-girl voice, such cute lines as, 'If we were married, I wouldn't take up much room.' And he tells her, 'Love is for the very young.' The naughty little girl, legs dangling out of the loft in the scene of their first meeting, has become the good, meek daughter. She has become his child.

The elision of the sexual and parental in this development is precisely the point – it is the sexuality of daughter–father relationships, and the dangerous sexual consequences of their disruption, that are played on in the Turner image and in the Georgia–Jonathan relationship. In turn, this relates to the theme of her becoming 'authentic'. Just as the car scene signals an explosion of 'real' feeling, so, too, with rather fewer stops pulled out, does the climax of the scene in her bedroom, where Jonathan smashes her father's 'shrine'. He has sneered at her – 'Look at you, you're acting now, playing the doomed daughter of the great man' – and when he smashes the shrine, she attacks him, her hair comes loose and swings in the light. In both cases, the 'real' feeling is signalled by a departure from the static, perfectly groomed look of Georgia/Turner to wild movement with textures (her hair here, her fur in the car scene) that capture and diffuse the light. And in both cases she is being required, forcibly, to reject her father (real or surrogate).

Whether she does succeed, however, in freeing herself from her second father, Jonathan – and hence, like the Turner image, from a father-fixated sexuality – is ambiguous. At the beginning of the film, just before she, together with Fred and James Lee, goes into Pebbel's office, she draws a moustache on the shield outside, Jonathan's emblem, exactly the same as the moustache he, Jonathan, draws on her father's portrait (later in the film, though earlier in her 'life'). She laughs with the others. This is clearly an act of defiance, doing to Jonathan what he did to her father. But perhaps it has to be read as only an act, not a real rejection. This is what the film suggests elsewhere. In the framing narrative she is dressed in black (a neat, tight-fitting suit), her hair drawn back. In the flashbacks, she wears light, usually white, clothes, and her hair hangs lustrously. The general contrast, and especially the cut back from the flashing car scene to her immobile, black figure, posed in recall, suggest repression. She is keeping unwanted desire in check, which is not the same thing as being free from it. She tells James Lee that one may grow out of first love, 'but you never get over it'. Directly, this means Jonathan, but, given the pattern of father references in the film, it could also mean her father – or fathers in general. Georgia has grown out of that (the 'mature' repression of desire in adulthood) but not got over it (still hung up on father figures). Of Turner, only the latter was touted as being the case. In the last shot of the film, she, like Fred and James Lee, remains fascinated by Jonathan, unable just to walk out, compelled to pick up the phone to hear what his ideas are. He still exercises his hold on her.

Whether this hold is a father–son one in the case of Fred and James Lee, I'm not sure. What does seem a reasonable supposition is that Jonathan himself is free of his own father. Despite keeping up appearances (paying mourners to attend his father's funeral), he befriends the only man, Fred, who speaks against his father, pronounces his father 'the heel' and seems to accept Georgia's father's view of him as a demon. He overthrows Pebbel, who is effectively in the position of his father, as head of the studio, and treats him with all the patronizing air of the still vigorous son. Jonathan is free of his father, but Georgia really is not. Perhaps this is because psychoanalytic thought only allows sons to kill fathers. Thus Georgia, like Turner, must remain pitiably locked into her perverse needs and desires.

Imitation of Life (1959)

By the time of *Imitation of Life* in 1959, the glamour emphasis in Turner's image had become uppermost. As Jeanine Basinger puts it, 'Turner appeared to cut loose her past. For the audience, it ceased to exist. She was their movie goddess – born and raised on film for their pleasure – the product of photogenesis' (1976: 17). The 'bad' elements continued before and after *Imitation of Life*, if anything more scandalous – four more marriages and divorces (Lex Barker 1953–7, Fred May 1960–2, Robert Eaton 1965–9, Ronald Dante 1969), accused of breaking up the marriage of Ava Gardner and Frank Sinatra her daughter's involvement in various scandals (drugs, becoming a stripper not to mention the Johnny Stompanato affair discussed below), and some film roles: *The Prodigal* (1955) as a wicked priestess, *Portrait in Black* (1960) as an adulterous murderer. However, the effect of all these was more to increase her glamorous otherness and to make her an identification figure the suffering woman of the woman's film genre. It is these qualities that *Imitation of Life* capitalizes upon. More precisely, it uses a quality of 'detachment' characterizing Turner's dress and acting styles.

Throughout the films and public appearances of the 1950s, and on into the 1960s, Turner became increasingly associated with clothes. The 1965 film *Love Has Many Faces* was sold principally on the strength of its 'million dollar wardrobe', and the connection between Turner and a certain kind of dress style was essential to the films she made for Ross Hunter (*Imitation of Life Portrait in Black, Madam X* (1966)). Although many different designers worked on her films, notably Edith Head (*Who's got the Action?* (1962), *Love Has Many Faces*), Jean Louis (*Imitation of Life, Portrait in Black, Madame X*) Helen Rose (*A Life of Her Own* (1950), *The Merry Widow* (1952), *The Bad and the Beautiful, Latin Lovers* (1953), *Bachelor in Paradise* (1961)) and Travilla (*The Rains of Ranchipur* (1955), *The Big Cube* (1969)), and although the style very clearly belongs to American 1950s *haute couture*, there is none the less a certain Lana Turner look. This is prominent in *Imitation of Life* and relates to the film's elaboration of what is implied by its title.

The signification of many of the features of the look are those of *haute couture* in general, notably expensiveness (especially, with Turner, jewellery, elaborate head-dresses and hair-dos) and, distinguishing the wearer from those whose clothes have to permit labour, inconvenience (for Turner, trains, elaborate folds in the skirt, off-the-shoulder dresses). Certain other features are more specifically Lana: the use of man-made fibres, so that her high style is associated with glossy, modern artifice rather than 'natural' or 'old-fashioned' values; a quality of hardness in the clear-cut edges of the designs and in the

use of colour, which, together with a tendency towards designs that create geo-
metrical patterns around her frame, 'dehumanizes' her, plays down qualities
of softness, roundness, even warmth; and a certain type of creation that is
frankly bizarre and unimaginable outside of movies, even of Turner, such as
an outfit in *Imitation of Life* consisting of vermilion pants and top, pink neck-
lace, and a piece of pink flower-printed, insubstantial material shaped like an
open-fronted dress, cut away at the knees, and trailing out behind in a full
spread (Figure 11.10). The emphasis, then, is on artifice (a feature of the
Turner image already dwelt upon), femininity (but one conceived not in terms
of softness, but in terms of elaborateness, ornamentation, plasticity) and sheer
impracticality, without connection with ordinary life. The net effect in many
of her films is that Turner, in her fabulous costumes, is visually detached from
her surroundings – India in *The Rains of Ranchipur*, Cornwall in *Another Time
Another Place* (1958), a rusty old steamship, captained by John Wayne, in *The
Sea Chase* (1955) – except in those cases where the set-up is itself equally
'unreal': as high priestess of Astarte in *The Prodigal* (revealing clothes that
make every movement hazardous), as the richest woman in the world in *Latin
Lovers* (in Brazil), and in *Love Has Many Faces* (in Acapulco). In *A Life of Her
Own* and *Peyton Place* (1957) she was associated directly with *haute couture* as,
respectively, a top model and owner of the town's smartest fashion salon.

The sense that all this gives to many of her film appearances – of her being
detached from the events, on show – is central in *Imitation of Life*, for in it
she plays a character, Lora, who is, or becomes, a person on show, performing,
presenting an image, to be thought of neither as an essence (i.e. an inner
human being expressing her self through presentation) nor as interacting
with others and circumstances. In the early scenes in the film, she wears
ordinary, everyday clothes – blouses and skirts, a suit for interview – but as
she gradually becomes an actor and a star, her wardrobe becomes more and
more Lana. If 'life' is essence, interaction, vitality, reality, then Lora/Turner,
in her outlandish outfits, is an imitation of it. The problem the film poses
(thus bringing in the suffering element in the Turner image) is whether there
is, in fact, anything but imitation in life.

The key metaphor for imitation in the film is that of acting. The fact that
Lora is an actor, in the professional sense, is only part of this. We never see
her on stage, except in rehearsal or taking a bow. In so far as her profession
is relevant to the metaphor of acting, it is in the way that she is set up as
'an actress' quite apart from any ability to act well on a stage. Thus agent
Allen Loomis takes her on because he is impressed by her impersonation of
an archetypal Hollywood star (this is how she inveigles her way into his
office) and he wants to promote her not by putting her into a play but by
taking her to parties *dressed like* an actress (in particular, in mink). Ironically,
the only time we get to know anything about a play she is in is when she
takes a part as a social worker in a bid for realism. But Lora/Turner acts,
puts on a performance, throughout the film. Detached by dress, she is further

Figure 11.10 Lanallure in *Imitation of Life*

detached by acting style. Turner has a habit – in her other later films as well – of turning away from the person she is acting with to deliver a line, adopting a posture, head-on to camera although not actually looking into the camera. Even when she does not do this, her acting none the less is poised and posed. If one takes as an example someone at the very opposite end of the scale to her, Judy Garland, one can observe how Garland hangs on her acting partner's every word, watching her/his lips or eyes, registering response in minute facial inflections. It is this that gives Garland's performances their characteristically nervy, tense and spontaneous feel. By contrast, Turner's beautifully made-up face moves very little and she does not even always look at her partner. All of this is emphasized time and again in *Imitation of Life*, until the climactic moment when, turning from her sobbing daughter Susie (Sandra Dee), she declares, staring ahead of her, that she will give up Steve (John Gavin) rather than have him come between them. Susie looks at her and says, 'Oh mother, stop acting!' The film here draws attention to Turner's posing acting style, making its use of the style to embody 'imitation' explicit.

This use of Turner was given a further emotional charge for contemporary viewers by Turner's involvement in the trial of her daughter Cheryl for the murder of her (Turner's) boyfriend Johnny Stompanato (in 1958). More than one newspaper described her testimony as 'the greatest performance of her life.' Whether or not this was fair of the press, the confusion was compounded by the purely coincidental release of *Peyton Place* around the time of the trial. In it, Turner's big scene has her breaking down in sobs on the witness stand, just as she did at the Stompanato trial. There are of course further overtones of the Stompanato affair in the relationship between Steve and Susie (just as rumour had it that Cheryl had fallen for Johnny), again blurring the distinction between imitation and reality, screen and life.

Acting is only one of the many images for imitation of life used by the film. All of these (for instance, a Nat King Cole substitute to sing the title song; the use of an obviously artificial, stage-set-like backdrop for Lora's home; narrative touches such as having a job writing envelopes to give them a wholly spurious 'personal touch') connect to the central metaphor of acting/performance, but unlike *The Bad and the Beautiful*, with its endless reflections and cross-references which trap everything in the paradoxes of illusionism, *Imitation of Life* does also point, in an ultimately very melancholic fashion, to the possibility, or idea, of authenticity.

In fact, nearly all the possibilities pointed to by the film are also pretty well undercut or attenuated by it. Christmas, vividly evoked with bright reds, snow and Christmas trees, is exposed as sham fairly devastatingly by Sarah Jane's materialist insistence that, since he was real, Christ must have been either black or white and by Annie (Juanita Moore) and Lora's idealist evasion in terms of it being the general idea of Christ that matters. Other possible authenticities are more ambiguously dealt with. I will look at them primarily as they relate to Lora/Turner.

The possibility of self-affirmation as a source of strength is most explored through the character of Sarah Jane (Susan Kohner) and her imitation of white, but the illusoriness of self-affirmation is underlined in the same way at certain points for both her and Lora. These ways are the use of mirror reflections at moments of affirmation and/or the introduction of the *Imitation of Life* theme on the soundtrack after such declarations. Thus when Lora rings Susie after her triumph in the role of Amy, her sense of fulfilment, achievement, is shown us only in a mirror image of it. (Compare Sarah Jane's fierce 'I'm white!' to a probing boyfriend, shown as reflected in a shop-window.)

Another possible source of authenticity is virility, here represented by Steve. Douglas Sirk often has a character like this in his films, embodying a promise of virility, to the women and impotent men of the rest of the cast – think of his use of Rock Hudson in *All That Heaven Allows, Written on the Wind* and *The Tarnished Angels*. The point about these characters – played by actors who are almost exaggeratedly tall, dark and handsome – is that their virility is never put to the test. They may offer the woman fulfilment (including, quite clearly, sexual fulfilment), but this remains speculative, to take place well after the end title has appeared. Sirk's films do not even end with the marriage of this male with the female protagonist, only with our assumption that this is the way all heterosexual romances end. Much less is the consummation assured. The ending of *Imitation of Life* is especially ambiguous. In one sense, it is the cobbling together of the nuclear family characteristic of the postwar film melodrama. That is to say that while we end with a nuclear family unit, it is actually made up from bits of other families (Steve is the father of neither girl; neither he nor Lora is Sarah Jane's parent). Moreover, it is shot not as father, mother and children grouped together, but as the women grouped together in the back of the car, with a cut-in shot of Steve looking on benignly from the front seat. In other words, the promise of virility that will set the seal on the family is still only a promise.

The problem with this is what exactly the film thinks of virility. Feminism has correctly exposed the oppressiveness of virility as an idea (as opposed to an idea such as energy or strength that need not be gender-specific), yet it does seem that *Imitation of Life*, and Sirk in his other films, do believe in virility as an idea. What is being critically exposed is the absence or failure of virility. In particular, the association of Steve with a certain view of the countryside (and even more a similar association between Rock Hudson and nature in *All That Heaven Allows*), seems to be presented quite straight, without undercutting, as if Sirk really believes in a natural order of virility and, possibly, the family, at least as ideals.

There is a similar problem with another of the film's alternatives to a life of imitation, namely black culture. The main lines of the Annie–Sarah Jane plot seem to be a repeat of the imitation themes in the Lora plot. The device of the black girl who can pass for white clearly demonstrates the thesis that race is a question of cultural definition, including role-playing, in which biological difference plays no significant part. Annie's investment of her self, her labour, in provision for her spectacular funeral, something which she herself by definition cannot experience, suggests the role of religious mystification in black culture. Yet the film also seems to want to say that black culture *is* more authentic than white, materially and culturally.

The role of Annie and Sarah Jane in the film is to act as the material base to the superstructure of Lora's success, which is mere phenomenal form. Annie almost lives Lora's real, practical life for her. She is the breadwinner (filling in envelopes, doing cleaning jobs, paying the bills) who enables Lora to pursue her career, and she is housewife and mother to Susie. She even at one point controls Lora's relationship with Steve, by gesturing him to go when she thinks Lora should be left alone. In other words, she is the reality, the material existence, that makes Lora's appearance possible. Moreover, it is quite clear that Lora has no conception of what it means to be black; she has no understanding of the reality that makes her life possible. She sees taking the part of the social worker as doing something more 'real' on the stage, yet cheerfully chats about its 'coloured angle' with David (Dan O'Herlihy) in front of Annie, without consulting *her*, without even seeming to register the fact that Annie is serving them drinks. When she upbraids Sarah Jane for her Southern mammy impersonation when bringing in drinks for her (Lora's) guests, she says, 'I've never treated you differently' – yet we have just seen Sarah Jane using the back stairs, going to the local school (Susie is at boarding-school), expected to help out her black servant mother. Lora has not consciously acted differently towards Sarah Jane and yet quite clearly Sarah Jane is getting different treatment. Lora has no conception of the racist structures that underpin her position and Sarah Jane's equally.

In addition to this materialist authenticity granted to blacks, the final funeral set-piece seems to affirm, its narrative significance *vis-à-vis* Annie's life notwithstanding, the cultural authenticity of blacks. Above all, the use of Mahalia Jackson (who really is Mahalia Jackson, not someone imitating her) suggests a core of real feeling in black religion. The fact that Jackson's singing is so 'genuinely' emotional that she cannot lip-synchronize herself with any precision draws attention to the artifice of the film medium which is 'unable' to 'capture' her untrammelled outpouring of emotion. Yet this final affirmation of the authenticity of black culture is also the high point of grief in the film. It is almost as if the film is saying that if there is anything other than imitation it is in suffering.

It is in relation to this that the use of Turner is most interesting, drawing as it does on both her 'artificial' and her 'suffering' image qualities. When Annie dies, Lora/Turner breaks down and cries, and it is as if some authentic feeling has broken through the hard shell of artifice elsewhere promoted by the film. It is worth comparing this with the car scene in *The Bad and the Beautiful*. In both cases, the effect is of Turner shedding her actor's artifices and giving us naked emotion. This may also be how Turner herself experienced it – we cannot know, and I do not wish to detract from her achievement in both cases. However, the effect also derives from the way both these scenes make a formal break from the rest of the film in the presentation of Turner. In *The Bad and the Beautiful*, the posed, static nature of her performance is replaced for the car scene by chaotic movement. In *Imitation of Life*, her collapse on Annie's bed makes one realize that as an element of composition everywhere else in the film, she has been used in upright and detached positions, usually still. The actual movement of falling on the bed breaks this, and the break is maintained through the funeral service where she is slumped at an angle in her seat. Whilst of course in both cases this is the art of the film-makers (of whom Turner is one) and whilst the notion of 'naked emotion' does not really have any validity, none the less this collapse into suffering, which is also a formal break in the film's compositional patterns *vis-à-vis* Turner, *means* 'authenticity', shedding of artifice, reality not imitation. What is melancholy is that this authenticity is achieved only in an image of collapse, as if the only possible reality behind the imitation of life is grief.

*   *   *

As I have been concerned in this article principally to discuss the star as an aspect of film language, I have tried generally to hold back from spelling out the ideological significance of Turner (and the star phenomenon), but a few words on this may be in order by way of a conclusion.

In this perspective the role of Turner as an agent of coherence (*Postman*) or to reinforce such notions as impulse (her marriages, *Postman*), naked emotion and authenticity (*The Bad and the Beautiful*, *Imitation of Life*) would not be viewed as progressive. At the same time, the way her image can disrupt a film text (the overall structure of *Ziegfeld Girl*, the centrality of Frank/Garfield to *Postman*) and its foregrounding of the processes of manufacture are suggestive. In a more directly political sense, it seems to me that her combination of sexuality and ordinariness was in itself ideologically explosive (and I have not sufficiently brought out the lower-class elements in this definition of ordinariness), comparable to that later embodied by Marilyn Monroe. To what extent the machinery of glamorization, punishment and suffering defused this, I'm not sure. I tend always to see ideological struggle within the texts of films, no less in Lana Turner than anywhere else.

Movie 25, 1977–8

Note

1   I should like to thank Jeremy Butler for drawing my attention to a number of textual inaccuracies in the original version of this article.

References

Alloway, Lawrence (1972) 'The iconography of the movies', in Ian Cameron (ed.) *Movie Reader*, London: November Books, 16–18.

Basinger, Jeanine (1976) *Lana Turner*, New York: Pyramid.

Cook, Jim (1977) '*On a Clear Day You Can See Forever*', Movie 24: 61–2.

Morella, Joe and Epstein, Edward Z. (1972) *Lana: The Life and Loves of Miss Turner*, London: W. H. Allen.

Further reading

Butler, Jeremy G. (ed.) (1991) *Star Texts: Image and Performance in Film and Television*, Detroit, MI: Wayne State University Press.

Fischer, Lucy (ed.) (1990) *Imitation of Life*, New Brunswick, NJ: Rutgers University Press.

Fischer, Lucy (1991) 'Lifestyles of the Rich and Famous: *Imitation of Life*', *Post Script* 10 (2), 5–13.

Gledhill, Christine (ed.) (1991) *Stardom: Industry of Desire*, London: Routledge.

Kaplan, E. Ann (ed.) (1978) *Women in Film Noir*, London: British Film Institute.

Lewis, Lisa A. (ed.) (1992) *The Adoring Audience: Fan Culture and Popular Media*, London and New York: Routledge.

12

FIRST A STAR

Elizabeth Taylor

'. . . we like vinegar with our greens – makes 'em taste better'
Rock Hudson to and of Elizabeth Taylor in *Giant*

Elizabeth Taylor was a Star before she was a Saint and both before she wa
a Dame.[1] Very few stars get to be either.

There are stars who have seemed to embody unalloyed virtue and decency
Mary Pickford, Lillian Gish, Henry Fonda, Gregory Peck, Julie Andrews
Many more have donated to charity and participated in the rounds of glitz
Hollywood fundraising, and indeed Taylor is of this company, even in 198
being awarded the Damon Runyon/Walter Winchell Humanitarian Awar
in recognition of her generosity. But it is not for this that she is a saint
Both Danny Kaye and Audrey Hepburn got closer to sainthood than many
going well beyond the call of photo opportunity duty in their work fo
UNESCO. No star, though, has quite put themselves on the line in suppor
of an initially despised cause as did Elizabeth Taylor with AIDS-related work
What's more, the power of this work springs from the very nature of stardom
not just in the sense of lending a famous name to a cause, but in the way i
seems to be a transmutation of the personal into the public. Taylor's AID
work is widely taken to spring from her loyal and abiding friendship wit
gay men – Roddy McDowell, Montgomery Clift, Rock Hudson (and perhap
we should throw in Michael Wilding and Judy Garland). This is the saint
liness of the devotion of friendship lived out publicly, starrily, as a courageou
commitment to an unpopular cause.

If very few stars become unofficial saints (none has yet been officiall
sanctified), not that many become knights or dames. Because it has mainl
been an award of high cultual prestige, many actors have of course been en
nobled, and in the sense that they are famous actors, they are stars. Howeve
you don't have to be a good actor to be a star. Stars are performers whos
presence fascinates, who interest us intensely for what we take them to be
As it happens, Elizabeth Taylor can be a very good actress. This has gener
ally been more readily recognized when she has shown herself able to rise t

the cultural level of her material, notably Edward Albee (*Who's Afraid of Virginia Woolf?* (1966)) and Tennessee Williams (*Cat on a Hot Tin Roof* (1958), *Suddenly Last Summer* (1959)). It's less often been noted when she has provided the spark of intelligent life to such films as *A Date with Judy* (1948), *Raintree County* (1957) and *Cleopatra* (1963). She is not reliably good – she is easily outclassed by the elephants in *Elephant Walk* (1954), while only Diana Rigg emerges honourably from *A Little Night Music* (1977). But in any case, whether good or bad, it is not for acting that a star is a star.

Nor is it simply for beauty, though for a love goddess this is a prerequisite. Taylor can indeed be breathtaking. In her first entrance in *A Place in the Sun* (1951), she walks down an open hallway into a gathering of people, talking away, radiating the confidence of her class and beauty; the camera rests in one position, letting her dominate the scene and the consciouness of the Montgomery Clift character. Later, when they have fallen in love, an extreme close-up of them (Figure 12.2) embracing has the top half of her face, seen over his shoulder, fill the screen, astonishingly luminous, the extreme paleness of her skin (pure white in this black-and-white film) offset by the jet blackness of her hair (and she is one the few white goddesses to have such dark hair without having a bad girl image). The image is repeated in two melancholy, lingering superimpositions at the end of the film, as Clift is led away to execution, having killed for love of her, an indelible mental impression of heart-stopping loveliness. Elizabeth Taylor was indeed a great beauty. All the same, that too is not enough for stardom; it needs to be offset by interest, even cut by something dissonant, the vinegar for the greens. With Elizabeth Taylor it is her voice.

This might not seem to be her greatest asset. It is high, thin, often squeaky or shrill. Most of the great women stars have voices either in a lower register (Garbo, Dietrich, Crawford, Stanwyck) or of an almost preternatural softness (Margaret Sullavan, Marilyn Monroe, Audrey Hepburn). They are voices of balm. Taylor's is nothing like this. Occasionally its tartness seems reined in, and then she seems dull and opaque – for part of what makes Taylor's fascinating performances fascinating is precisely this sharp little voice in that sumptuous body.

At times it sounds common and can even lend a cheap, sulky look to her lips. Given her well-to-do English parentage and her frequent casting as a rich girl, this is all the more surprising, and enchanting. Her untouchable, rich-are-different air becomes engaging, sympathetic, not-so-different. This is shored up by the many stories about her that suggest a down-to-earth quality alongside the glamour. When she and Gina Lollobrigida turned up at the 1961 Moscow Film Festival wearing the identical 'exclusive' Dior frock, she thought it hilarious while Lollobrigida was furious. When she flashed the 33.19 carat, $300,000-plus Krupp diamond that Richard Burton gave her in 1968, she said, 'I know I'm vulgar, but would you have me any other way?' Asked how she, one of the most beautiful women in the world,

Figure 12.1 Wanting something else: Elizabeth Taylor in *Cat on a Hot Tin Roof*

Figure 12.2 Extreme close-up: Elizabeth Taylor and Montgomery Clift in *A Place in the Sun*

felt about appearing as a hideous witch for part of *The Blue Bird* (1975), she invited anyone to come round any morning early, she always looked like that then. These are endearing stories, that heighten her beauty even as they make it less remote.

The voice adds edge, cutting the blandness of loveliness. It is especially apt to suggest needy desire and its frustration, and also a sense of something indefinable and unnamable about what is desired. The voice carries what may be read into aspects of both her 'private' life and her screen roles. The succession of husbands, the drama of divorce and remarriage often intensified by tragedy (the death of Mike Todd in an air crash), scandal ('stealing' Eddie Fisher away from Debbie Reynolds) and farce (the Burton saga), suggests someone determined to have a good time but also hints that the good time is perhaps never quite found. Similarly in many roles you don't quite know why or what her character wants with such insistence – in films like *Rhapsody* (1954), *A Place in the Sun* or *Raintree County*, she keeps telling the man how much she loves him, yet the voice seems to want something else. This is not the wifely love of a June Allyson, nor the sensuality of an Ava Gardner – within the conventions of the time, these are both properly feminine, both concerned with male pleasure, the one with looking after, the other with showing a good time. Elizabeth Taylor's voice, though, wants something

115

Figure 12.3 Preternaturally lovely: Paul Newman and Elizabeth Taylor in *Cat on a Ho*
   Tin Roof

else, her own pleasure, only what that is cannot be spoken or even knowr
Perhaps it is the voice of the clitoris in an age which spoke only of the peni
and vagina.

This is why, at her most memorable, she is so achingly alive. There is
feral quality to her enactment of passionate equine attachment in *Nationa*
Velvet (and how astonishing to think that she's been a star ever since, that is
since 1944); she is a deliciously selfish and vain Amy in *Little Women* (1949)
In both *Cat on a Hot Tin Roof* and *Reflections in a Golden Eye* (1967), she plays
incandescently, women married to homosexual men. In a pair of films mad
back to back, *Giant* (1956) and *Raintree County*, she plays a woman cultur
ally displaced through marriage (respectively, a New Englander in Texas an
a Southern belle in a Northern town), kicking against the pricks of hide

116

bound views of women, courage and dignity always threatening to be undermined by shrillness.

Sometimes a role and a star seem made for each other. In *Cat*, Paul Newman says to her, 'Lady, that finishing school voice of yours sounds like you was running upstairs to tell someone the house was on fire.' She's classy but panicky, sensuous but jumpy with frustrations, like, as she says in reply, a cat on a hot tin roof. Cats are gorgeous creatures, capable of purring but also whining and screeching, adorable but selfish, even adorably selfish. Most of Elizabeth Taylor's performances, on and off screen, hint at this perennial fascination, at once sexually alluring and sympathetically recognizable. This is why, saint or dame, she is also first a star.

Note

1   This article was commissioned for a publication (which was never realized) to accompany the exhibition on Elizabeth Taylor at the National Portrait Gallery in London in 2000 on the occasion of her being made a Dame.

Further reading

Walker, Alexander (1966) 'Star syndrome: Elizabeth Taylor', in *The Celluloid Sacrifice*, London: Michael Josesph, 131–45.

13

THE SON OF THE SHEIK

The term 'sex object' implies a certain passivity, a person just 'there' for the viewer to gaze upon. Sex objects are pinned up, fixed, to be looked at. This submissiveness accords easily with the female sex role, which is so heavily defined in terms of passivity; but what happens when it is a man who is the sex object? *The Son of the Sheik* is an interesting example of some of the ways a film can deal with having a man as the object of the camera's and the viewer's adoration.

The camera certainly does adore Valentino as Ahmed in this film. His smooth, Latin-dark skin glows like satin under the studio lighting. He is always the most important element in the composition, whether because of the way he is placed, or because of his eye-catching costumes, or because of the intensity of his movements.

In addition to this loving treatment, the film clearly sets him up as the epitome of male beauty by a sustained contrast with two other characters who are also defined by their bodies, the comically lustful dwarf and the phoney strong man at the Café Maure. Like his, their bodies are a spectacle: but whereas his is a synthesis of sexuality and strength, their bodies are grotesque parodies of one or other of these qualities. These two figures are constantly framed in relation to Ahmed, in a way that serves to heighten his sensual bodily perfection.

Such sustained sexual objectification does not mean, however, that the film contains a role reversal, with a man the object of a woman's desire in exactly the same way that, in films, women normally are of men's desires. Yasmin is seen in the film before Ahmed, and he is introduced as the object of her desire – but the way it is done is crucial. In the usual case, the male hero *sees* the woman, and there is a shot of her as he sees her – it is a shot that looks like a pin-up, like a passive object of desire. In *The Son of the Sheik*, Yasmin *thinks* about Ahmed and then there is a (flashback) shot of him – he is already located in her dreams, a spiritual realm of desire. Moreover, it is a shot of him *looking at her* dancing, looking with an eye-narrowed intensity that counteracts any notion that she might be looking at him. He is, in other words, an extremely active object of desire.

Figure 13.1 Glinting with desirability: Valentino in *The Son of the Sheik*

This goes for the whole film. He is a conventional active hero figure: his dashing adventures and swordplay are part of what makes him attractive According to the film, female sexual desire consists of 'experiencing' a man rather than pursuing him. It is his penetrating gaze, his driving energy, that are supposed to be the turn-on, culminating in ravishment.

But it is not a rape fantasy. There is no indication that Yasmin is supposed to have enjoyed being taken by force. The morning after, there are only shots of her in tears and him looking remorseful. Rape as enjoyment of being overwhelmed may be the logical conclusion of the way the film has set up women's sexual pleasure in men, but it actually holds back from that conclusion. Ahmed and Yasmin go on loving each other *despite* their violent sexual encounter, not because of it.

Ahmed's treatment of Yasmin also precipitates a row with his father, a classic Oedipal moment, a contest over the definition of correct sexual conduct. Father and son are reconciled only in the final scene, which is essentially a fight over Yasmin's honour. In between, there has been a conversation between the Sheik and his wife Diana, in which she has reminded him of his own hot-blooded ways as a youth – in *The Sheik* (1921). Just as the Sheik has grown up, so he must help his son to grow up, and the Oedipal pattern of conflict preceding the son's taking his father's place in society is repeated This conflict between men is the real subject of the whole second half of the film, making the question of Yasmin and what she wants much less important.

The most curious aspect of the film is the relation between the setting and the characters. All act as stock Arab figures, such as sheiks and belly-dancers and they act out a rather stark drama of sexual morality. Yet most of the main characters are not Arabs but Europeans (English and French) who live as Arabs. In this way *The Son of the Sheik* comes to feel like the 'secret life' of contemporary western society, an exploration of the then otherwise unspeakable subjects of female desire, rape and father–son conflict. The audience could take it two ways. Shocked by the sexual explicitness, it could dismiss the depicted events 'anthropologically' as foreign behaviour. Drawn into the characters, however, it could welcome the film as a sunlit dream of sexuality. In a period not yet saturated in Freudian ideas, such dreams were still possible.

The Movie 126, 198.

Further reading

Hansen, Miriam (1991) 'Pleasure, ambivalence, identification: Valentino and female spectatorship', in Christine Gledhill (ed.) *Stardom: Industry of Desire*, London: Routledge, 259–82.

Leconte, Loredana (1996) 'Fascino Latino: l'invenzione di Rodolfo Valentino' in Malossi, Giannino (ed.) *Latin Lover: A sud della passione*, Milan: Charta, 81–93.

Studlar, Gaylyn (1989) 'Discourses of gender and ethnicity: the construction and de(con)struction of Rudolph Valentino as other', *Film Criticism* 13 (2), 18–35.

14

DON'T LOOK NOW

The instabilities of the male pin-up

'One of the things I really envy about men,' a friend once said to me, 'is the right to look.' She went on to point out how in public places, on the street, at meetings, men could look freely at women, but that women could only look back surreptitiously, against the grain of their upbringing. It is a point that has been reiterated in many of the personal political accounts that have emerged from the consciousness-raising of the women's movement. And it is a fact that we see endlessly reworked in movies and on television. We have all seen, countless times, that scene of Young Love, where, in the canteen, at school, in church, the Boy and the Girl first see each other. The precise way it is done is very revealing. We have a close-up of him looking off camera, followed by one of her looking downwards (in a pose that has, from time immemorial, suggested maidenliness). Quite often, we move back and forth between these two close-ups, so that it is very definitely established that he looks at her and she is looked at. Then, she may look up and off camera, and we may go back briefly to the boy still looking – but it is only briefly, for no sooner is it established that she sees him than we must be assured that she at once averts her eyes. She has seen him, but she doesn't look at him as he looks at her – having seen him, she quickly resumes being the one who is looked at.

So utterly routine is this kind of scene that we probably don't remark on it, yet it encapsulates, and effectively reinforces, one of the fundamental ways by which power relations between the sexes are maintained. In her book *Body Politics*, Nancy M. Henley examines the very many different non-verbal ways that gender roles and male power are constantly being rebuilt and reaffirmed. She does for gesture, body posture, facial expressions and so on what Dale Spender's *Man Made Language* does for verbal communication, and shows how non-verbal communication is both a register of male–female relations and one of the means by which those relations are kept the way they are. Particularly relevant here is her discussion of eye contact.

Henley argues that it is not so much a question of whether women or men look at each other, but how they do. In fact, her evidence suggests that in face-to-face interactions, women look at men more than men do at women

– but then this is because women listen more to men, pay more attention to them. In other words, women do not so much look at men as watch them. On the other hand, in crowd situations, men look more at women – men stare at women, whereas women avert their eyes. In both cases, this (re-) establishes male dominance. In the first case (one-to-one), 'superior position ... is communicated by visually ignoring the other person – *not* looking while listening, but looking into space as if the other isn't there'; whereas in the second case (crowds), 'staring is used to *assert* dominance – to establish, to maintain, and to regain it' (1977: 166).

Images of men aimed at women – whether star portraits, pin-ups, or drawings and paintings of men – are in a particularly interesting relation to these eye contact patterns. A certain instability is produced – the first of several we encounter when looking at images of men that are offered as sexual spectacle. On the one hand, this is a visual medium, these men are there to be looked at by women. On the other hand, this does violence to the codes of who looks and who is looked at (and how), and some attempt is instinctively made to counteract this violation. Much of this centres on the model or star's own 'look' – where and how he is looking in relation to the woman looking at him, in the audience or as she leafs through the fan or women's magazine (not only *Playgirl*, which has male nudes as *Playboy* has female ones, but also teenage magazines like *Oh Boy!* and *My Guy*, with their half-dressed pin-ups, and such features as 'Your Daily Male' in the *Sun* and 'She-Male' in *She*) (Figure 14.1).

To repeat, it is not a question of whether or not the model looks at his spectator(s), but how he does or does not. In the case of not looking, where the female model typically averts her eyes, expressing modesty, patience and a lack of interest in anything else, the male model looks either off or up. In the case of the former (Figure 14.2), his look suggests an interest in something else that the viewer cannot see – it certainly doesn't suggest any interest in the viewer. Indeed, it barely acknowledges the viewer, whereas the woman's averted eyes do just that – they are averted from the viewer. In the cases where the model is looking up, this always suggests a spirituality (Figure 14.3): he might be there for his face and body to be gazed at, but his mind is on higher things, and it is this upward striving that is most supposed to please. This pose encapsulates the kind of dualism that Paul Hoch analyses in his study of masculinity, *White Hero, Black Beast* – higher is better than lower, the head above is better than the genitals below. At the same time, the sense of straining and striving upwards does also suggest analogies with the definition of the very sexuality supposedly relegated to an inferior place – straining and striving are the terms most often used to describe male sexuality in this society.

It may be, as is often said, that male pin-ups more often than not do not look at the viewer, but it is by no means the case that they never do. When they do, what is crucial is the kind of look it is, something very often deter-

Page Three
FELLA

LONDONER Jamie Arnold beefed up his biceps with regular doses of iron – the weight-training variety that is.

JAMIE is also in strict training to get his vocal chords in shape to go solo as a singer. He has already appeared in pop videos.

Picture:
PAUL
MASSEY

DON'T L
Fi
YOU must
the skinn
leotard v
hours ev
Her joints are o
injuries, and she

Figure 14.2 Looking off: Rudolph Valentino

Figure 14.1 (Facing page) 'Mirror Fella', 11 January 1990

Figure 14.3 Looking up: Montgomery Clift

Figure 14.4 Looking through: Paul Newman

mined by the set of the mouth that accompanies it. When the female pin-up returns the viewer's gaze, it is usually some kind of smile, inviting. The male pin-up, even at his most benign, still stares at the viewer. Even Paul Newman's frank face-on to the camera (Figure 14.4) or the *Oh Boy!* coverboy's yearning gaze at us still seems to reach beyond the boundary marked, when the photo was taken, by the camera, as if he wants to reach beyond and through and establish himself. The female model's gaze stops at that boundary, the male's looks right through it.

Freud noticed a similar sort of look on Michelangelo's statue of Moses – though Moses is not looking at us but at the Jews' worship of the Golden Calf. Since Freud, it is common to describe such a look as 'castrating' or 'penetrating' – yet to use such words to describe the look of a man at a woman is revealing in ways that Freudians do not always intend. What, after all, have women to fear from the threat of castration? And why, come to that, should the possibility of penetration be *necessarily* fearful to women? It is clear that castration can only be a threat to men, and more probable that it is the taboo of male anal eroticism that causes masculine-defined men to construct penetration as frightening and the concept of male (hetero)sexuality as 'taking' a woman that constructs penetration as an act of violence. In looking at and dealing with these castrating/penetrating looks, women are caught up in a system that does not so much address them as work out aspects of the construction of male sexuality in men's heads.

If the first instability of the male pin-up is the contradiction between the fact of being looked at and the attempt of the model's look to deny it, the second is the apparent address to women's sexuality and the actual working out of male sexuality (and this may be one of the reasons why male pin-ups notoriously don't 'work' for women). What is at stake is not just male and female sexuality, but male and female power. The maintenance of power underpins further instabilities in the image of men as sexual spectacle, in terms of the active/passive nexus of looking, the emphasis on muscularity and the symbolic association of male power and the phallus.

The idea of looking (staring) as power and being looked at as powerlessness overlaps with ideas of activity/passivity. Thus to look is thought of as active; whereas to be looked at is passive. In reality, this is not true. The model prepares her or himself to be looked at, the artist or photographer constructs the image to be looked at; and, on the other hand, the image that the viewer looks at is not summoned up by his or her act of looking but in collaboration with those who have put the image there. Most of us probably experience looking and being looked at, in life as in art, somewhere among these shifting relations of activity and passivity. Yet it remains the case that images of men must disavow this element of passivity if they are to be kept in line with dominant ideas of masculinity-as-activity.

For this reason images of men are often images of men doing something. When, before the full invention of cinematography, Eadweard Muybridge took an enormous series of photographic sequences, each one in the sequence taken a few seconds after the other, one of his intentions was to study the nature of movement. Muybridge photographed sequences of naked male and female figures. In a study of these sequences, Linda Williams (1981) shows how, even in so 'scientific' an undertaking and at such a comparatively 'primitive' stage in the development of photography, Muybridge established a difference between the female subjects, who are just there to be looked at, and the male subjects, who are doing something (carrying a boulder, sawing wood, playing baseball) which we can look in on. This distinction is maintained in the history of the pin-up, where time and again the image of the man is one caught in the middle of an action, or associated, through images in the pictures, with activity.

Even when not actually caught in an act, the male image still promises activity by the way the body is posed. Even in an apparently relaxed, supine pose, the model tightens and tautens his body so that the muscles are emphasized, hence drawing attention to the body's potential for action (Figure 14.5). More often, the male pin-up is not supine anyhow, but standing taut ready for action.

There is an interesting divergence here in ethnic and class terms, a good example of the way that images of male power are always and necessarily inflected with other aspects of power in society. In relation to ethnicity, it is generally the case that the activity shown or implied in images of white men is clearly related to the split in western society between leisure and work activity, whereas black men, even though they are in fact American or European, are given a physicality that is inextricably linked to notions of 'the jungle', and hence 'savagery'. This is done either by a natural setting, in which a generalized physical exertion is conflated with the energies of nature (and, doubtless, the beat of drums), or else, more recently, in the striking use of 'black power' symbolism (Figure 14.6). This might seem like an acknowledgement of ethnic politics, and perhaps for some viewers it is, but the way the media constructed black power in fact tended to reproduce the idea of a savage energy rather than a political movement – hence the stress on back-to-Africa (in the white western imagination still an amorphous jungle), or the 'senseless' violence erupting from the jungle of the ghetto.

Such images also put black men 'outside of' this class (though there has been the promotion of specifically middle-class black images, as with, especially, Sidney Poitier). White men are more likely to be class differentiated, but this does overlap with the work/leisure distinction. Work is in fact almost suppressed from dominant imagery in this society – it is mainly in socialist imagery that its images occur. In nineteenth-century socialist and trade union art and in Soviet socialist realism the notions of the dignity and heroism of labour are expressed through dynamically muscular male bodies. As Eric Hobsbawm (1978) has pointed out, what this tradition has done, in effect, is to secure for masculinity the definition of what is finest in the proletarian

Figure 14.5
Supine but taut
for *Playgirl*

Figure 14.6 Black power as sex appeal: Billy Dee Williams

and socialist traditions – women have been marginalized to the ethereal role of 'inspiration'. Moreover, it is certainly no *conscious* part of this tradition that these male bodies should be a source of erotic visual pleasure, for men and women.

Sport is the area of life that is the most common contemporary source of male imagery – not only in pin-ups of sportsmen, but in the sports activities of film stars, pop stars and so on. (*She* magazine ran a series of pin-ups of wrestlers.) Although certain sports have very clear class associations (the Prince of Wales plays polo, not football), there is a sense in which sport is a 'leveller'. Running, swimming, ball games are pretty well open to anyone in any class, and so imagery derived from these activities does not have immediate class associations. What all imply, however, is leisure, and the strength and vitality to use it. The celebration of the body in sport is also a celebration of the relative affluence of western society, where people have time to dedicate themselves to the development of the body for its own sake.

Whether the emphasis is on work or sport or any other activity, the body quality that is promoted is muscularity. In the copy accompanying the pin-ups in *Oh Boy!*, for instance, the female readers are called on to 'getta load of his muscles' and other such invitations. Although the hyper-developed muscularity of an Arnold Schwarzenegger is regarded by most people as excessive, and perhaps bordering on the fascist (Figure 14.7), it is still the case that muscularity is a key term in appraising men's bodies. This again probably comes from men themselves. Muscularity is the *sign* of power – natural, achieved, phallic.

At a minimum, developed muscles indicate a physical strength that women do not generally match (although recent developments in women's sport and physical conditioning suggest that differences between the sexes here may not be so fixed). The potential for muscularity in men is seen as a biological given, and is also the means of dominating both women and other men who are in the competition for the spoils of the earth – and women. The point is that muscles are biological, hence 'natural', and we persist in habits of thought, especially in the area of sexuality and gender, whereby what can be shown to be natural must be accepted as given and inevitable. The 'naturalness' of muscles legitimizes male power and domination (Figure 14.8).

However, developed muscularity – muscles that *show* – is not in truth natural at all, but is rather achieved. The muscle man is the end-product of his own activity of muscle-building. As always, the comparison with the female body beautiful is revealing. Rationally, we know that the beauty queen has dieted, exercised, used cleansing creams, solariums and cosmetics – but none of this really shows in her appearance, and is anyway generally construed as something that has been *done to* the woman. Conversely, a man's muscles constantly bespeak this achievement of his beauty/power.

Muscles, as well as being a sign of activity and achievement, are hard. We've already seen how even not overly developed male pin-ups harden their

Figure 14.7 Bodybuilding and the Third World: Arnold Schwarzenegger

Figure 14.8 Muscles and the naturalization of male power in *Viva* for women

Figure 14.9 Hysterical iconography: Humphrey Bogart 'at home'

Figure 14.10 Looking awkward for *Playgirl*

bodies to be looked at. This hardness may then be reinforced by aspects of setting or symbolic references, or by poses that emphasize hard lines and angular shapes (not the soft roundness of the feminine aesthetic). In her book *The Nude Male*, Margaret Walters suggests this hardness is phallic, not in the direct sense of being like an erect penis but rather in being symbolic of all that the phallus represents of 'abstract paternal power'. There is no doubt that the image of the phallus as power is widespread to the point of near universality, all the way from tribal and early Greek fertility symbols to the language of pornography, where the penis is endlessly described as a weapon a tool, a source of terrifying power.

There is a danger of casual thought here. The phallus is not just an arbi trarily chosen symbol of male power; it is crucial that the penis has provided the model for this symbol. Because only men have penises, phallic symbols even if in some sense possessed by a woman (as may be the case with female rulers, for instance), are always symbols of ultimately male power. The woman who wields 'phallic' power does so in the interests of men.

This leads to the greatest instability of all for the male image. For the fact is that the penis isn't a patch on the phallus. The penis can never live up to the mystique implied by the phallus. Hence the excessive, even hysterical quality of so much male imagery. The clenched fists, the bulging muscles the hardened jaws, the proliferation of phallic symbols – they are all straining after what can hardly ever be achieved, the embodiment of the phallic mystique (Figure 14.9). This is even more the case with the male nude. The limp penis can never match up to the mystique that has kept it hidden from view for the last couple of centuries, and even the erect penis often looks awkward, stuck on to the man's body as if it is not a part of him (Figure 14.10).

Like so much else about masculinity, images of men, founded on such multiple instabilities, are such a strain. Looked at but pretending not to be, still yet asserting movement, phallic but weedy – there is seldom anything easy about such imagery. And the real trap at the heart of these instabilities is that it is precisely *straining* that is held to be the great good, what makes a man a man. Whether head held high reaching up for an impossible transcendence or penis jerking up in a hopeless assertion of phallic mastery, men and women alike are asked to value the very things that make masculinity such an unsatisfactory definition of being human.

Screen 23 (3–4), 1982

References

Henley, Nancy M. (1977) *Body Politics*, Englewood Cliffs, NJ: Prentice-Hall.
Hobsbawm, Eric (1978) 'Man and woman in socialist iconography', *History Workshop Journal* 6: 121–38.
Hoch, Paul (1979) *White Hero, Black Beast*, London: Pluto Press.
Spender, Dale (1980) *Man Made Language*, London: Routledge & Kegan Paul.
Walters, Margaret (1978) *The Nude Male*, London: Paddington Press.
Williams, Linda (1981) 'Film body: an implantation of perversions', *Cinétracts* 3 (4): 19–35.

Further reading

Brauerhoch, Annette (1986) 'Glanz und elend der muskelmänner', *Frauen und Film* 40: 20–6.
Cooper, Emmanuel (1989) *The Sexual Perspective*, London: Routledge & Kegan Paul.
Green, Ian (1984) 'Malefunction', *Screen* 25 (4–5): 36–49.
Kent, Sarah (1985) 'The erotic male nude', in Sarah Kent and Jacqueline Morreau (eds) *Women's Images of Men*, London: Writers & Readers Publishing, 75–105.
McKinnon, Kenneth (1997) *Uneasy Pleasures: The Male as Erotic Object*, London: Cygnus Arts.
Mercer, Kobena and Julien, Isaac (1988) 'Race, sexual politics and black masculinity', in Rowena Chapman and Jonathan Rutherford (eds) *Male Order*, London: Lawrence & Wishart, 97–164.
Moore, Suzanne (1988) 'Here's looking at you, kid!', in Lorraine Gamman and Margaret Marshment (eds) *The Female Gaze*, London: Women's Press, 44–59.
Neale, Steve (1983) 'Masculinity as spectacle', *Screen* 24 (6): 2–16.
Waugh, Thomas (1996) *Hard To Imagine: Gay Male Eroticism in Photography and Film from Their Beginnings to Stonewall*, New York: Columbia University Press.

15

COMING TO TERMS
Gay pornography

The main suggestions I'd like to make in this essay about gay male porno-graphic cinema are quite brief and simple. Broadly I'm going to argue that the narrative structure of gay porn[1] is analogous to aspects of the social construction of both male sexuality in general and gay male sexual practice in particular. But before getting on to that it seems necessary to say a few things by way of introduction. Pornography has recently become a Big Topic in left cultural work,[2] and what I'm going to say needs to be situated in relation to this.

First, a definition – a working definition, the one I'm going to be working with here, rather than a statement of the correct definition of pornography. I want some definition that is as broadly descriptive as possible. Discussion about porn tends to start off by being either for or against all porn and to be caught up in equally dubious libertarian or puritanical ideas. I don't mean to imply that I believe in the myth of objectivity, that I start off utterly neutral. I'm a gay man, who has (unlike women) easy access to porn and can take pleasure in it,[3] but who feels a commitment to the more feminist inflec-tions of gay male politics. I'm also a socialist who sees porn as capitalist production but does not believe all capitalist cultural production always all the time expresses capitalist ideology (cf. Lovell 1980). I'm constantly looking for moments of contradiction, instability and give in our culture, the points at which change can be effected, and want to start out with the possibility of finding it in porn as anywhere else. So the definition I'm going to use is that a pornographic film is *any* film that has as its aim sexual arousal in the spectator.

This definition makes porn film a familiar kind of genre, that is, one that is based on the effect that both producers and audiences know the film is supposed to have. It is not defined (or I am not asking to define it here), like the Western, gangster film, or musical, by such aesthetic, textual elements as iconography, structure, style and so on, but by what it produces in the spectator. It is like genres such as the weepie and the thriller, and also low or vulgar comedy. Like all of these, it is supposed to have an effect that is registered in the spectator's body – s/he weeps, gets goose-bumps, rolls about laughing, comes. Like these genres, porn is usually discussed in relation to a similar, but 'higher' genre which doesn't have a bodily effect – weepies (melodramas and soap opera) are compared to tragedy or realist drama, thrillers to mystery/detective stories (based on intellectual, puzzle-solving narratives), low comedy (farce) to high comedy (comedy of manners), and porn to erotica.

I'd like to use porn as a neutral term, describing a particular genre. If one defines porn differently, then the kind of defence of porn as a genre (but emphatically not of most porn that is actually available) that I'm involved with here is not really possible. Feminist critiques of pornography (e.g. Dworkin 1981, Griffin 1981, Lederer 1980) rightly stress the degradation of women that characterizes so much heterosexual porn, and these critiques in fact define pornography as woman-degrading representations of sexuality. Although feeling closer to some of those feminist articles that take issue with this hardline anti-porn position (Myers 1982, Allen and Harris 1982, Winship 1982, Rich 1982), I do not feel as out of sympathy with, say, Andrea Dworkin's work as many people, and especially gay men, that I know. Although in relation to gay porn Dworkin is in some respects inaccurate (e.g. in stressing gay porn's use of socially inferior – young, black – men in 'feminine' positions, whereas similarity between partners is more often the case) or out of date (Allen and Harris 1982: 22), her rage at what so much of porn consists of is fully justified, and especially so because she effectively defines porn as that which is degrading and out*rage*ous. But I'd like all the same to hang on to a wider notion of sexual representation, and still use the word pornography precisely because of its disreputable, carnal associations. (Maybe the feminist debate means that I can't use the word like this – but I don't want to fall for the trap of substituting the word erotica.[4])

The fact that porn, like weepies, thrillers and low comedy, is realized in/through the body has given it low status in our culture. Popularity these genres have, but arbiters of cultural status still tend to value 'spiritual' over 'bodily' qualities, and hence relegate porn and the rest to an inferior cultural position.

One of the results of this is that culturally validated knowledge of the body, of the body's involvement in emotion, tends to be intellectual knowledge about the body, uninformed by experiential knowledge of it.[5] Let me try to be clear about this. I'm not saying that there can be a transparent, pure knowledge of the body, untouched by historical and cultural reality. On the contrary, all knowledge is culturally and historically specific, we do not transcend our material circumstances. We learn to feel our bodies in particular ways, not 'naturally'. But an intellectual or spiritual knowledge about the body is different from experiential knowledge of the body – both are socially constructed, but the latter is always in a dynamic material and physical relationship with the body, is always knowledge in and of the body. Intellectual or spiritual knowledge on the other hand divorces social construction from that which it constructs, divorces knowledge about the body from knowing with the body. (Certain types of discourse analysis – but by no means all – clearly fall into the same idealist trap.[6])

Moreover, the effect of the cultural status of intellectual/spiritual accounts of the body is to relegate experiential knowledge of the body to a residual category. Of course idealist discourse accounts do not allow any such category at all.[7] Thus experiential knowledge (except when sanctified by the subjugation of the body in most forms of 'physical education') is allowed to be both inferior and just a given, not socially constructed,[8] to be just 'experience', not socially constructed experiential knowledge. By valuing the spiritual, the bodily is left as something natural, and sexuality as the most natural thing of all. What is in fact also socially constructed (experiential knowledge of the body, and of sexuality) is not recognized as such, and for that reason is not reflected upon, is allowed to go its supposed own way until it meets up with spiritual censors. Even gay theory and feminist theory have been notoriously reluctant to think through the social construction of the body without lapsing into the Scylla of Lacanian psychoanalysis (where social construction does not construct anything *out of* any material reality) and the Charybdis of both gay liberationist let-it-all-hang-out (where sexuality is a pure impulse awaiting release) and the implicit sexual essentialism of radical feminist ideas of masculine aggression and women's power (cf. Wilson 1983).

A defence of porn as a genre (which, I repeat, is not at all the same thing as defending most of what porn currently consists of) would be based on the idea that an art rooted in bodily effect can give us a knowledge of the body that other art cannot.

Even now porn does give us knowledge of the body – only it is mainly bad knowledge, reinforcing the worst aspects of the social construction of masculinity that men learn to experience in our bodies. All the same, porn can be a site for 're-educating desire' (Carter 1981) and in a way that constructs desire in the body, not merely theoretically in relation to, and often against, it.

To do that, though, means rejecting any notion of 'pure sex', and particularly the defence of porn as expressing or releasing a sexuality 'repressed by bourgeois (etc.) society. This argument has gained some ground in gay male circles, and with good reason. Homosexual desire has been constructed as perverse and unspeakable; gay porn does speak/show gay sex. Gay porn asserts homosexual desire, it turns the definition of homosexual desire on its head, says bad is good, sick is healthy and so on. It thus defends the universal human practice of same sex physical contact (which our society constructs as homosexual); it has made life bearable for countless millions of gay men.

But to move from there to suggest that what we have here is a natural sexuality bursting out of the confines of heterosexual artificial repression is much more of a problem.

This is certainly the way that Gregg Blachford's article 'Looking at pornography' (1988) can be read, and seems to be the contention behind David Ehrenstein's article 'Within the pleasure principle, or irresponsible homosexual propaganda' (1980). The latter[9] argues that porn movies, unlike mainstream films that imply sexuality but don't show it, give us the pure pleasure of voyeurism which lies unacknowledged behind all cinema.

> The pornographic is obvious, absolute, unmistakable – no lies or omissions or evasions can hold quarter in its sphere.

Porn is the 'abandon of everything to the pleasure principle' (ibid.: 65) conceptualized as pure drive (the more usual appropriation of Freudian ideas than the Lacanian version influential in academic film studies circles). Porn itself operates with this idea, and the view is clearly expressed in the introduction to *Meat* (McDonald 1981), a collection of writings from the magazine *Straight to Hell*. The magazine, like the book, consists entirely of personal accounts of gay sexual experience sent in to the magazine by gay men. I have no reason to suppose that the accounts are not genuine both in the sense of having actually been sent in (not ghost-written) and of describing real experiences. But this 'genuineness' is not to be conflated, as book and magazine do, with the notion of an unconstructed sexuality – raw, pure and so on. A reading of *Meat*, or a look at gay porn, indicates really rather obviously that the sexuality described/represented is socially meaningful. Class, ethnicity and of course concepts of masculinity and gayness/straightness all clearly mark these gay pornographic productions: and indeed the very stress on sexuality as a moment of truth, and its conceptualization as raw, pure, etc., is itself historically and culturally produced (Foucault 1980).

What makes *Meat* and gay movie-house porn especially interesting and important is the extent to which they blur the line between representation and practice. *Meat* is based on (I think largely) true encounters that really happened. Watching porn in gay cinemas usually involves having sex as well – not just self-masturbation but sexual activity with others, in a scenario brilliantly evoked by Will Aitken (1981–2) in his article 'Erect in the dark'. In principle then gay porn is a form of representation that can be the site and occasion for the production of bodily knowledge of the body. In this definition, porn is too important to be ignored, or to be left to the pornographers.

Narrative manifestation

I'd like now to turn to one of the ways in which the education of desire that porn is involved in is manifested, namely its use of narrative.[10]

It is often said that porn movies as a genre are characterized by their absence of narrative. The typical porn movie, hard core anyway, is held to be an endless series of people fucking, and not even, as Beatrice Faust notes, fucking in the 'normal' physiological order that Masters and Johnson have 'recorded' (1982: 16). Gay porn (and indeed what hetero porn I have seen), however, is full of narrative. Narrative is its very basis.

Even the simplest pornographic loops have narrative. In those quarter-in-the-slot machines where you just get a bit of a porn loop for your quarter, you are very conscious of what point (roughly) you have come into the loop, you are conscious of where the narrative has got to. Even if all that is involved is a fuck between two men, there are the following narrative elements: the arrival on the scene of the fuck, establishing contact (through greeting and recognition, or through a quickly established eye-contact agreement to fuck), undressing, exploring various parts of the body, coming, parting. The exploration of the body often involves exploring those areas less heavily codified in terms of sexuality, before 'really getting down to/on with' those that are (genitals and anus). Few short porn films don't involve most or all of these narrative elements, and in that order. Usually too there is some sort of narrative detail – in *Muscle Beach* (Figure 15.1), one man (Rick Wolfmier) arrives on the scene (a beach) in a truck, the other man (Mike Betts) is already there sunbathing; Wolfmier walks by the sea for a while; there is quite a long sequence of shot:reverse shot cutting as they see each other and establish contact; self-masturbation precedes their actual physical contact with each other; after orgasm, Wolfmier and Betts drive away together in the truck. Already then minimal character elements are present, of not inconsiderable social interest – the iconography of the truck, the looks of the two men, the culture of the beach and of bodybuilding, and so on.

Even when the film is yet more minimal than this, there is still narrative – and essentially the same narrative, too. Some gay porn loops simply show one man masturbating. A rather stylish version of this is *Roger*, which just has the eponymous star masturbating. The music is a kind of echoing drumbeat; there is no set to speak of; the lighting is red, covering the screen in varieties of pulsating hue; the film cuts between long shots and medium shots in a quite rhythmic way, often dissolving rather than cutting clean. It will be clear that there is something almost abstract or avant-gardeish about the film, as the cinematic means play visually with its solo subject, Roger masturbating. Yet even here there is a basic narrative – Roger enters, masturbates, comes. (Where you put your quarter in might mean that *you* start with his orgasm and run on to where he comes in; but you'd know and be able to reconstruct the proper narrative order that your quarter has cut across.)

Even in so minimal and abstract a case, there is narrative – *Roger* is a classic goal-directed narrative. The desire that drives the porn narrative forward is the desire to come, to have an orgasm. And it seems to me that male sexuality, homo or hetero, is socially constructed, at the level of representation anyway, in terms of narrative; that, as it were, male sexuality is itself understood narratively.

Figure 15.1 Bodybuilding and romance: *Muscle Beach*

The goal of the pornographic narrative is coming; in filmic terms, the goal is ejaculation, that is, visible coming. If the goal of the pornographic protagonist (the actor or 'character') is to come, the goal of the spectator is to see him come (and, more often than not, to come at the same time as him). Partly this has to do with 'proof', with the form's 'literalness', as Beatrice Faust puts it, with the idea that if you don't really see semen the performer could have faked it (and so you haven't had value for money). But partly too it has to do with the importance of the visual in the way male sexuality is constructed/conceptualized. It is striking how much pornographic literature, not a visual medium, stresses the visible elements of sex. (Most remarkable perhaps is Walter, the Victorian narrator of *My Sweet Life*, with his obsessive desire to see into his partner's vagina, even to the detail of seeing, for instance, what his semen looks like after he has ejaculated it into her vagina.) Men's descriptions of their own erections seldom have to do with how their penises feel, but with how they look. The emphasis on seeing orgasm is then part of the way porn (re)produces the construction of male sexuality.

Could it be otherwise, could sexuality be represented differently? So dominant are masculine-centred definitions of sexuality that it often seems as if all representations of sexuality (pornographic or otherwise) are constructed as driven narrative. But there are alternatives, and one that struck me was the lesbian sequence at the end of *Je tu il elle*, directed by Chantal Akerman. (As Margaret Mead pointed out, you need only one example of things being different to establish that things can be different in the organization of human existence and hence that things can be changed.) The sequence itself is part of a (minimalist) narrative; but taken by itself it does not have the narrative drive of male porn. It starts *in media res* – there is no arrival in the room the women are already making love when the sequence stars (though the previous shot has, perhaps ambiguously, established that they are going to make love); there is no sense of a progresssion to the goal of orgasm; nor is there any attempt to find visual or even (as in hetero porn?) aural equivalents for the visible male ejaculation. In particular, there is no sense of genital activity being the last, and getting-down-to-the-real-thing, stage of the experience. It is done in three long takes – no editing cuts across a sexual narrative (as in gay porn; see below); the harsh white lighting and the women's white bodies on crumpled white sheets in a room painted white, contribute to the effect of representing the sexuality as more dissolving and ebbing than a masculine thrusting narrative. Let me stress that I am *not* talking about what the women are doing – for much of the time their actions are far more snatching and grabbing than, for instance, the generally smooth, wet action of fellatio in gay porn. My point is the difference in narrative organization in the cinematic representation of sexuality.[11]

I am not suggesting that this is a better representation of sexuality, or the correct mode for representing lesbian sexuality. Also I want to bracket the question of whether the difference between the two modes of representation is based on biological differences between female and male sexuality, or on different social constructions of sexuality, or on a combination of the two.[12] All I want to get over is the difference itself, and the fact that male porn, whether homo or hetero, is ineluctably caught in the narrative model. (This is particularly significant in hetero porn in that it is predominantly constructed around a female protagonist (Giles 1976), who is attributed with this narrativized sexuality. However, I am not about to get into whether this is a gain – a recognition of female sexuality as desire – or a loss – a construction of female sexuality in male terms.)

The basis of gay porn film is a narrative sexuality, a construction of male sexuality as the desire to achieve the goal of a visual climax. In relation to gay sexual politics, it is worth signalling that this should give pause to those of us who thought/hoped that being a gay man meant that we were breaking with the gender role system. At certain levels this is true, but there seems no evidence that in the predominant form of how we represent our sexuality to ourselves (in gay porn) we in any way break from the norms of male sexuality.

Particularly significant here is the fact that although the pleasure of anal sex (that is, of being anally fucked) is represented, the narrative is never organized around the desire to be fucked, but around the desire to ejaculate (whether or not following on from anal intercourse). Thus although at the level of public representation gay men may be thought of as deviant and disruptive of masculine norms because we assert the pleasures of being fucked and the eroticism of the anus (Hocquenghem 1978), in our pornography this takes a back seat.[13]

This is why porn is politically important. Gay porn, like much of the gay male ghetto, has developed partly out of the opening up of social spaces achieved by the gay liberation movements; but porn and the ghetto have overwhelmingly developed within the terms of masculinity. The knowledge that gay porn (re)produces must be put together with the fact that gay men (like straight men but unlike women) do have this mode of pubic sexual expression available to them, however debased it may be. Like male homosexuality itself, gay porn is always in this very ambiguous relationship to male power and privilege, neither fully within it nor fully outside it (cf. Barrett 1980: 42–84, *passim*). But that ambiguity is a contradiction that can be exploited. In so far as porn is part of the experiential education of the body, it has contributed to and legitimized the masculine model of gay sexuality, a model that always implies the subordination of women. But rather than just allowing it to carry on doing so, it should be our concern to work against *this* pornography by working with/within pornography to change it – either by interventions within pornographic film-making itself (Siebenand 1980), or by the development of porn within the counter-cinemas (always remembering that the distinction between porn in the usual commercial sense and sexual underground/alternative/independent cinema has always been blurry when you come to look at the films themselves), or by criticism that involves audiences reflecting on their experience of pornography (rather than by closing down on reflection by straight condemnation or celebration of it).

So far all I've been talking about is the most basic, minimal narrative organization of (gay) male pornography. However, gay porn is characterized as much by the elaborations of its narrative method as by its insistence on narrative itself. Though the bare narrative elements may often not go beyond those described above, they are frequently organized into really quite complex narrative wholes. Often there is a central narrative thread – two men who are in love or who want to get off with each other – but this is punctuated by almost all of the devices of narrative elaboration imaginable, most notably flashbacks (to other encounters, or previous encounters of the main characters with each other), fantasies (again, with others or each other, of what might or could be), parallelism (cutting back and forth between two or more different sexual encounters) and so on. All preserve the coming-to-visual-climax underlying narrative organization, but why this fascination with highly wrought narrative patterns? To begin with, of course, it is a way of getting more fucks in, with more people (Mele and Thirkell 1981). There is even perhaps an element of humour, as the film-makers knowingly strain their imagination to think of ways of bringing in yet more sex acts. But it is also a way of teasing the audience sexually, because it is a way of delaying climax, of extending foreplay. In parallel sequences, each fuck is effectively temporally extended, each climax is delayed. More generally, the various additional encounters delay the fulfilment of the basic narrative of the two men who are the central characters. (For example, in *L.A. Tool and Die* the underlying narrative is Wylie's journey to Los Angeles to find a job and his lover Hank; Wylie and Hank are played by the stars of the film, Will Seagers and Richard Locke, so we know that their having sex together must be the climax; but there are various encounters along Wylie's way, including memories, observation of other couples, incidental encounters with other men, and even inserted scenes with characters with whom Wylie has no connection, before arrival at Los Angeles and finally making it with Hank.)

There is a third reason for this narrative elaboration. Just as the minimal coming-to-visual-climax structure is a structural analogue for male sexuality, so the effective multiplication of sex acts through elaborate narrativity is an analogue for a (utopian) model of a gay sexual lifestyle that combines a basic romanticism with an easy acceptance of promiscuity. Thus the underlying narrative is often romantic, the ultimate goal is to make love with *the* man; but along the way a free-ranging, easy-going promiscuity is possible. While not all gay men actually operate such a model of how they wish to organize their affective lives, it is a very predominant one in gay cultural production, a utopian reconciliation of the desire for romance *and* promiscuity, security *and* freedom, making love *and* having sex.

It is worth stressing how strong the element of romance is, since this is perhaps less expected than the celebration of promiscuity. The plot of *L.A. Tool and Die* outlined above is a good example, as is *Navy Blue* in which two sailors on shore leave seek out other lovers because each doesn't think that the other is gay, yet each is really in love with the other (as fantasy sequences make clear) – only at the end of the film do they realize their love for each other. Or take *Wanted*, a gay porn version of *The Defiant Ones*, in which two convicts, one gay (Al Parker) and one straight (Will Seagers), escape from prison together. Despite Seagers's hostility to Parker's sexuality, they stick together, with Parker having various sexual encounters, including watching Seagers masturbate. The film is a progression from the sadistic prison sexuality at the start (also offered, I know, as pornographic pleasure), through friendly mutual sexual pleasuring between Parker and various other men, to a final encounter, by an idyllic brookside, between Parker and Seagers which is the culmination of their developing friendship. Some men I know who've seen the film find this final sequence too conventionally romantic (which it is – that's why I like it) or else too bound up with the self-oppressive fantasy of the straight man who deigns to have sex with a fag. It can certainly be taken that way, but I know when I first saw it I was really moved by what seemed to be Seagers's realization of the sexuality of his feeling for Parker. And what particularly moved me was the moment when Seagers comes in Parker's mouth, and the latter gently licks the semen off Seagers's penis, because here it seemed was an explicit and arousing moment of genital sexuality that itself expressed a tender emotional feeling – through its place in the narrative, through the romanticism of the setting, through the delicacy of Parker's performance. If porn taught us *this* more often . . .

One of the most interesting ways of making narratives complex in gay porn is the use of films within films. Many gay porn films are about making gay porn films, and many others involve someone showing gay porn films to himself or someone else (with the film-within-the-film then becoming for a while the film we are watching). The process of watching, and also of being watched (in the case of those films about making gay porn), is thus emphasized, not in the interests of foregrounding the means of construction in order to deconstruct them, but because the pleasure of seeing sex is what motivates (gay) male pornography and can be heightened by having attention drawn to it. (There is a whole other topic, to do with the power in play in looking/being looked at, which I won't get into here.) We have in these cases a most complex set of relations between screen and auditorium. On screen someone actually having sex is watched (photographed) by a film-maker watched (photographed) by another invisible film-maker (the one who made the film on screen), and all are watched by someone in the audience who is (or generally reckons to be) himself actually having sex. Gay porn here collapses the distinction between representation and that which it is a representation of, while at the same time showing very clearly the degree to which

representation is part of the pleasure to be had even in that which it is a
representation of. Porn (all porn) is, for good or ill (and currently mainly for
ill), part of how we live our sexuality; how we represent sexuality to ourselves
is part of how we live it, and porn has rather cornered the market on the
representation of sexuality. Gay porn seems to make that all the clearer,
because there is greater equality between the participants (performers, film-
makers, audiences)[14] which permits a fuller exploration of the education of
desire that is going on. Porn involves us bodily in that education: criticism
of porn should be opening up reflection on the education we are receiving
in order to change it.

Jump Cut 30, 1985

Acknowledgement

I'd like to thank *Jump Cut* editorial collective for their helpful and also very
enjoyable involvement in the editing of this article. Since first writing it I
have incorporated not only many of their suggestions but also much of the
useful discussion on pornography and gay macho in the Birmingham Gay
Men's Socialist Group. Many thanks to all these people, then – but I'll still
take the blame for the finished article.

Notes

1 For the rest of the article, 'gay porn' will always refer to gay *male* porn.
2 For a general introduction to this, see Lesage (1981) and the bibliography in
   Marchetti (1981).
3 This access is not actually so easy outside of certain major metropolitan centres and
   police practices in Great Britain hit gay porn far more decisively than straight.
4 'Because it is less specific, less suggestive of actual sexual activity, "erotica" is regu-
   larly used as a euphemism for "classy porn". Pornography expressed in literary
   language or expensive photography and consumed by the upper middle class is
   "erotica"; the cheap stuff, which can't pretend to any purpose but getting people off,
   is smut.' Ellen Willis, quoted in Carter (1981: 20–38).
5 An example of this is the role of the representation of the body in Christian iconography. At one level, the body of Christ could not be a more central motif of
   Christianity, most notably in the image of Christ on the cross. But the tendency
   remains to stress what the body means at the expense of what it is, to highlight
   transcendence over the body. In the Christian story of Christ as the Word made flesh
   it is the Word that ultimately matters, not the flesh.
6 The magazine *m/f* is the leading example of this.
7 For a critique of idealism, Lovell (1980).
8 The one area of cultural work that has been concerned with body knowledge is dance
   but the leading exponents of Modern Dance such as Isadora Duncan and Ruth St
   Denis have been influentially committed to notions of natural movement. See Kendall
   (1979).

9 I am conscious that because this article, in a manner of speaking, attacks things I have written – and even attacks what it infers from them about my sexual practices – I may here treat the article rather unfairly.

10 This is only one element of any full analysis. One of the major elements not discussed here, and that needs work doing on it, is the role of iconography – of dress and setting, and especially performers, the male types that are used, porn stars' images and so on, all drenched in ideological meanings.

11 For further discussion see Martin (1980).

12 For a discussion of this difficult nature/nurture debate from a socialist feminist perspective that does not discount the contribution of biology altogether, see Sayers (1982).

13 Waugh (1985) disputes the assertion in this paragraph.

14 This is a question of degree – producers and audiences are not equal in their power of determining the form that representation takes, and especially in a field so fiercely colonized by capitalist exploitation as pornography; and at the psychological level, performers and audience members are not necessarily equal, in that performers are validated as attractive sexual beings to a degree that audience members may not be. But the point is that they are all gay men participating in a gay sub-culture, a situation that does not hold with heterosexual porn. See Siebenand (1980) and Waugh (1985).

References

Aitken, Will (1981–2) 'Erect in the dark', *Gay News* (Winter Extra December/January): 15–20.

Allen, Deborah and Harris, Gavin (1982) 'Languages of rage and revenge', *Gay Information* 9/10: 20–7.

Barrett, Michèle (1980) *Women's Oppression Today*, London: Verso.

Blachford, Gregg (1978) 'Looking at pornography', *Gay Left* 6: 16–20

Carter, Mick (1981) 'The re-education of desire: some thoughts on current erotic visual practices', *Art and Text* 4: 20–38.

Dworkin, Andrea (1981) *Pornography: Men Possessing Women*, New York: Putnam's.

Ehrenstein, David (1980) 'Within the pleasure principle, or irresponsible homosexual propaganda', *Wide Angle* 4 (1): 62–5.

Faust, Beatrice (1982) *Women, Sex and Pornography*, Harmondsworth, Middlesex: Penguin.

Foucault, Michel (1980) *The History of Sexuality*, Vol. 1, trans. Robert Hurley, New York: Vintage.

Giles, Dennis (1976) 'Angel on fire', *Velvet Light Trap* 16.

Griffin, Susan (1981) *Pornography and Silence*, London: Women's Press.

Hocquenghem, Guy (1978) *Homosexual Desire*, London: Allison & Busby.

Kendall, Elizabeth (1979) *Where She Danced*, New York: Alfred Knopf.

Lederer, Laura (ed.) (1980) *Take Back the Night*, New York: William Morrow.

Lesage, Julia (1981) 'Women and pornography', *Jump Cut* 26: 46–7, 60.

Lovell, Terry (1980) *Pictures of Reality*, London: British Film Institute.

McDonald, Boyd (ed.) (1981) *Meat*, San Francisco, CA: Gay Sunshine Press.

Marchetti, Gina (1981) 'Readings on women and pornography', *Jump Cut* 26: 56–60.

Martin, Angela (1980) 'Chantal Akerman's films: a dossier', *Feminist Review* 3: 24–47.

Mele, Sam and Thirkell, Mark (1981) 'Pornographic narrative', *Gay Information* 6: 10–13.

Myers, Kathy (1982) 'Towards a feminist erotica', *Camerawork* 24: 14–16, 19.

Rich, B. Ruby (1982), review of the film *Not a Love Story, Village Voice*, 20 July.

Sayers, Janet (1982) *Biological Politics*, London: Tavistock.

Siebenand, Paul Alcuin (1980) *The Beginnings of Gay Cinema in Los Angeles: the Industry and the Audience*, Ann Arbor, MI: University of Michigan Press.

Waugh, Thomas (1985) 'Men's pornography: gay vs straight', *Jump Cut* 30: 30–6.

Wilson, Elizabeth (1983) *What Is To Be Done About Violence Against Women?* Harmondsworth, Middlesex: Penguin.

Winship, Janice (1982), review of Andrea Dworkin (1981) *Pornography: Men Possessing Women, Feminist Review* 11: 97–100.

Further reading

Burger, John R (1995) *One-Handed Histories: The Eroto-Politics of Gay Male Video Pornography*, New York: Harrington.

Dyer, Richard (2001) 'Idol thoughts: orgasm and self-reflexivity in gay pornography' in *The Culture of Queers*, London: Routledge.

Fung, Richard (1988) 'Looking for my penis: the eroticised Asian in gay video porn' in Bad Object Choices (ed.) *How Do I Look?*, Seattle: Bay Press, 148–60.

Henderson, Lisa (1992) 'Lesbian pornography: cultural transgression and sexual demystification', in Sally Munt (ed.) *New Lesbian Criticism*, London: Harvester, 173–91.

Merck, Mandy (1993) '*More of a Man*: gay porn cruises gay politics' in *Perversions*, London: Virago, 217–35.

Patton, Cindy (1988) 'The cum shot: three takes on lesbian and gay sexuality', *Outlook* 1 (3): 72–7.

Ross, Andrew (1989) *No Respect: Intellectuals and Popular Culture*, New York and London: Routledge.

Watney, Simon (1987) *Policing Desire*, London: Comedia/Methuen.

Waugh, Thomas (1983) 'A heritage of pornography', *The Body Politic* 90: 29 33.

Waugh, Tom (1996) *Hard to Imagine: Gay Male Eroticism in Photography and Film from Their Beginnings to Stonewall*, New York: Columbia University Press.

Williams, Linda (1990) *Hard Core: the Frenzy of the Visible*, Berkeley, CA: University of California Press.

16

IN DEFENCE OF DISCO

All my life I've liked the wrong music. I never liked Elvis and rock'n'roll; I always preferred Rosemary Clooney. And since I became a socialist, I've often felt virtually terrorized by the prestige of rock and folk on the left. How could I admit to two Petula Clark LPs in the face of miners' songs from the north-east and the Rolling Stones? I recovered my nerve partially when I came to see showbiz-type music as a key part of gay culture, which, whatever its limitations, was a culture to defend. And I thought I'd really made it when I turned on to Tamla Motown, sweet soul sounds, disco. Chartbusters already, and I like them! Yet the prestige of folk and rock, and now punk and (rather patronizingly, I think) reggae, still holds sway. It's not just that people whose politics I broadly share don't *like* disco, they manage to imply that it is politically beyond the pale to like it. It's against this attitude that I want to defend disco (which otherwise, of course, hardly needs any defence).

I'm going to talk mainly about disco *music*, but there are two preliminary points I'd like to make. The first is that disco is more than just a form of music, although certainly the music is at the heart of it. Disco is also kinds of dancing, club, fashion, film, etc., in a word, a certain *sensibility*, manifest in music, clubs, etc., historically and culturally specific, economically, technologically, ideologically and aesthetically determined – and worth thinking about. Second, as a sensibility in music it encompasses more than what we would perhaps strictly call disco music, to include a lot of soul, Tamla and even the later work of 'Easy Listening' artistes like Peggy Lee and Johnny Mathis.

My defence is in two parts. First, a discussion of the arguments against disco in terms of its being 'capitalist' music. Second, an attempt to think through the – ambivalently, ambiguously, contradictorily – positive qualities of disco.

Disco and capital

Much of the hostility to disco stems from the equation of it with capitalism. Both in how it is produced and in what it expresses, disco is held to be irredeemably capitalistic.

151

Now it is unambiguously the case that disco is produced by capitalist industry, and since capitalism is an irrational and inhuman mode of production, the disco industry is as bad as all the rest. Of course. However, this argument has assumptions behind it that are more problematic. These are of two kinds. One assumption concerns *music as a mode of production*, and has to do with the belief that it is possible in a capitalist society to produce things (e.g. music, e.g. rock and folk) that are outside of the capitalist mode of production. Yet quite apart from the general point that such a position seeks to elevate activity outside of existing structures rather than struggles against them, the two kinds of music most often set against disco as a mode of production are not really convincing.

One is folk music – in Britain, people might point to Gaelic songs and industrial ballads – the kind of music often used, or reworked, in left fringe theatre. These, it is argued, are not, like disco (and pop music in general), produced for the people but by them. They are 'authentic' people's music. So they are – or rather, were. The problem is that we don't live in a society of small, technologically simple communities such as produce such art. Preserving such music at best gives us an historical perspective on peasant and working-class struggle, at worst leads to a nostalgia for a simple, harmonious community existence that never really existed. More bluntly, songs in Gaelic or dealing with nineteenth-century factory conditions, beautiful as they are, don't mean much to most English-speaking people today.

The other kind of music most often posed against disco and 'pap pop' at the level of how it is produced is rock (including Dylan-type folk and everything from early rock 'n' roll to progressive concept albums). The argument here is that rock is easily produced by non-professionals – all that is needed are a few instruments and somewhere to play – whereas disco music requires the whole panoply of recording studio technology, which makes it impossible for non-professionals (the kid in the streets) to produce. The factual accuracy of this observation needs supplementing with some other observations. Quite apart from the very rapid – but then bemoaned by some purists – move of rock into elaborate recording studios, even when it is simple produceable by non-professionals, the fact is that rock is still quite expensive, and remains in practice largely the preserve of middle-class people who can afford electric guitars, music lessons, etc. (You have only to look at the biographies of those now professional rock musicians who started out in a simple non-professional way – the preponderance of public school and university educated young men in the field is rivalled only by their preponderance in the Labour Party front bench.) More importantly, this kind of music production is wrongly (except perhaps at certain key historical moments) thought of as being generated from the grass roots – non-professional music making, in rock as elsewhere, bases itself, inevitably, on professional music. Any notion that rock emanates from 'the people' is soon confounded by the recognition that what 'the people' are doing is trying to be as much like professionals as possible.

The second kind of argument based on the fact that disco is produced by capitalism concerns *music as an ideological expression*. Here it is assumed that capitalism as a mode of production necessarily and simply produces 'capitalist' ideology. The theory of the relation between the mode of production and the ideologies of a particular society is too complicated and unresolved to be gone into here, but we can begin by remembering that capitalism produces commodities, and its interest in commodities is their exchange-value (how much profit they can realize) rather than their use-value (their social or human worth). This becomes particularly problematic for capitalism when dealing with an expressive commodity – such as disco – since a major problem for capitalism is that there is no necessary or guaranteed connection between exchange-value and use-value – in other words, capitalism as productive relations can just as well make a profit from something that is ideologically opposed to bourgeois society as something that supports it. As long as a commodity makes a profit, what does it matter? (I should like to acknowledge my debt to Terry Lovell for explaining this aspect of capitalist cultural production to me.) Indeed, it is because of this dangerous, anarchic tendency of capitalism that ideological institutions – the Church, the state, education, the family, etc. – are necessary. It is their job to make sure that what capitalism produces is in capitalism's longer-term interests. However, since they often don't know that that is their job, they don't always perform it. Cultural production within capitalist society is then founded on two profound contradictions: the first, between production for profit and production for use; the second, within those institutions whose job it is to regulate the first contradiction. What all this boils down to, in terms of disco, is that the fact that disco is produced by capitalism does not mean that it is automatically, necessarily, simply supportive of capitalism. Capitalism constructs the disco experience, but it does not necessarily know what it is doing, apart from making money.

I am not now about to launch into a defence of disco music as some great subversive art form. What the arguments above lead me to is, first, a basic point of departure in the recognition that cultural production under capitalism is necessarily contradictory, and, second, that it may well be the case that capitalist cultural products are most likely to be contradictory at just those points – such as disco – where they are most commercial and professional, where the urge to profit is at its strongest. Third, this mode of cultural production has produced a commodity, disco, that has been taken up by gays in ways that may well not have been intended by its producers. The anarchy of capitalism throws up commodities that an oppressed group can take up and use to cobble together its own culture. In this respect, disco is very much like another profoundly ambiguous aspect of male gay culture, camp. It is a 'contrary' use of what the dominant culture provides, it is important in forming a gay identity, and it has subversive potential as well as reactionary implications.

The characteristics of disco

Let me turn now to what I consider to be the three important characteristics of disco – eroticism, romanticism and materialism. I'm going to talk about them in terms of what it seems to me they mean within the context of gay culture. These three characteristics are not in themselves good or bad (any more than disco music as a whole is), and they need specifying more precisely. What is interesting is how they take us to qualities that are not only key ambiguities within gay male culture, but have also traditionally proved stumbling blocks to socialists.

Eroticism

It can be argued that all popular music is erotic. What we need to define is the specific way of thinking and feeling erotically in disco. I'd like to call it 'whole body' eroticism, and to define it by comparing it with the eroticism of the two kinds of music to which disco is closest – popular song (i.e. the Gershwin, Cole Porter, Burt Bacharach type of song) and rock.

Popular song's eroticism is 'disembodied': it succeeds in expressing a sense of the erotic which yet denies eroticism's physicality. This can be shown by the nature of tunes in popular songs and the way they are handled.

Popular song's tunes are rounded off, closed, self-contained. They achieve this by adopting a strict musical structure (AABA) in which the opening melodic phrases are returned to and, most importantly, the tonic note of the whole song is also the last note of the tune. (The tonic note is the note that forms the basis for the key in which the song is written; it is therefore the harmonic 'anchor' of the tune and closing on it gives precisely a feeling of 'anchoring', coming to a settled stop.) Thus although popular songs often depart – especially in the middle section (B) – from their melodic and harmonic beginnings, they also always return to them. This gives them – even at their most passionate, say, Porter's 'Night and Day' – a sense of security and containment. The tune is not allowed to invade the whole of one's body. Compare the typical disco tune, which is often little more than an endlessly repeated phrase which drives beyond itself, and is not 'closed off'. Even when disco music uses a popular song standard, it often turns it into a simple phrase. Gloria Gaynor's version of Porter's 'I've Got You Under My Skin', for instance, is in large part a chanted repetition of 'I've got you'.

Popular song's lyrics place its tunes within a conceptualization of love and passion as emanating from 'inside', the heart or the soul. Thus the yearning cadences of popular song express an erotic yearning of the inner person, not the body. Once again, disco refuses this. Not only are the lyrics often more

154

directly physical and the delivery more raunchy (e.g. Grace Jones's 'I Need a Man'), but, most importantly, disco is insistently rhythmic in a way that popular song is not.

Rhythm, in western music, is traditionally felt as being more physical than other musical elements such as melody, harmony and instrumentation. This is why western music is traditionally so dull rhythmically – nothing expresses our Puritan heritage more vividly. It is to other cultures that we have had to turn – and above all to Afro-American culture – to learn about rhythm. The history of popular song since the late nineteenth century is largely the history of the white incorporation (or ripping off) of black music – ragtime, the Charleston, the tango, swing, rock'n'roll, rock. Now what is interesting about this incorporation/ripping-off is what it meant and means. Typically, black music was thought of by the white culture as being both more primitive and more 'authentically' erotic. Infusions of black music were always seen as (and often condemned as) sexual and physical. The use of insistent black rhythms in disco music, recognizable by the closeness of the style to soul and reinforced by such characteristic features of black music as the repeated chanted phrase and the use of various African percussion instruments, means that it inescapably signifies (in this white context) physicality.

However, rock is as influenced by black music as disco is. This then leads me to the second area of comparison between disco's eroticism and rock's. The difference between them lies in what each 'hears' in black music. Rock's eroticism is thrusting, grinding – it is not whole body, but phallic. Hence it takes from black music the insistent beat and makes it even more driving; rock's repeated phrases trap you in their relentless push, rather than releasing you in an open-ended succession of repetitions as disco does. Most revealing perhaps is rock's instrumentation. Black music has more percussion instruments than white, but it knows how to use them to create all sorts of effect – light, soft, lively, as well as heavy, hard and grinding. Rock, however, only hears the latter and develops the percussive qualities of essentially non-percussive instruments to increase this, hence the twanging electric guitar and the nasal vocal delivery. One can see how, when rock'n'roll first came in, this must have been a tremendous liberation from popular song's disembodied eroticism – here was a really physical music, and not just mealy-mouthedly physical, but quite clear what it was about – cock. But rock confines sexuality to cock (and this is why, no matter how progressive the lyrics and even when performed by women, rock remains indelibly phallocentric music). Disco music, on the other hand, hears the physicality in black music and its range. It achieves this by a number of features including: the sheer amount going on rhythmically in even quite simple disco music (for rhythmic clarity with complexity, listen to the full-length version of the Temptations' 'Papa was a Rolling Stone'); the willingness to play with rhythm, delaying it, jumping it, countering it rather than simply driving on and on (examples: Patti Labelle, Isaac Hayes); the range of percussion instruments used and with different affects (e.g. the spiky violins in Quincy Jones/Herbie Hancock's 'Tell Me a Bedtime Story': the gentle pulsation of George Benson). This never stops being erotic, but it restores eroticism to the whole of the body, and for both sexes, not just confining it to the penis. It leads to the expressive, sinuous movement of disco dancing, not just that mixture of awkwardness and thrust so dismally characteristic of dancing to rock.

Gay men do not intrinsically have any prerogative over whole body eroticism. We are often even more cock-oriented than non-gays of either sex, and it depresses me that such phallic forms of disco as Village People should be so gay identified. None the less, partly because many of us have traditionally not thought of ourselves as being 'real men' and partly because gay ghetto culture is also a space where alternative definitions, including of sexuality, can be developed, it seems to me that the importance of disco in scene culture indicates an openness to a sexuality that is not defined in terms of cock. Although one cannot easily move from musical values to personal ones, or from personal ones to politically effective ones, it is at any rate suggestive that gay culture should promote a form of music that denies the centrality of the phallus while at the same time refusing the non-physicality which such a denial has hitherto implied.

Romanticism

Not all disco music is romantic. The lyrics of many disco hits are either straightforwardly sexual – not to say sexist – or else broadly social (e.g. Detroit Spinners' 'Ghetto Child', Stevie Wonder's 'Living in the City'), and the hard drive of Village People or Labelle is positively anti-romantic. Yet there is none the less a strong strain of romanticism in disco. This can be seen in the lyrics, which often differ little from popular song standards, and indeed often are standards (e.g. 'What a Difference a Day Made' – Esther Phillips, 'La Vie en Rose' – Grace Jones). More impressively, it is the instrumentation and arrangements of disco music that are so romantic.

The use of massed violins takes us straight back, via Hollywood, to Tchaikovsky, to surging, outpouring emotions. A brilliant example is Gloria Gaynor's 'I've Got You Under My Skin', where in the middle section the violins take a hint from one of Porter's melodic phrases and develop it away from his tune in an ecstatic, soaring movement. This 'escape' from the confines of popular song into ecstacy is very characteristic of disco music and nowhere more consistently than in such Diana Ross classics as 'Reach Out' and 'Ain't No Mountain High Enough'. This latter, with its lyrics' total surrender to love, its heavenly choir and sweeping violins, is perhaps one of the most extravagant reaches of disco's romanticism. But Ross is also a key figure in the gay appropriation of disco.

What Ross's records do – and I'm thinking basically of her work up to *Greatest Hits* volume 1 and the *Touch Me in the Morning* album – is express the intensity of fleeting emotional contacts. They are all-out expressions of adoration which yet have built in to them the recognition of the (inevitably) temporary quality of the experience. This can be a straightforward lament for having been let down by a man, but more often it is both a celebration of a relationship and the almost willing recognition of its passing and the exquisite pain of its passing:

> Remember me
> As a sunny day
> That you once had
> Along the way . . .

> If I've got to be strong
> Don't you know I need to have tonight when you're gone
> When you go I'll lie here
> And think about
> The last time that you
> Touch me in the morning.

This last number, with Ross's 'unreally' sweet, porcelain, fragile voice and the string backing, concentrates that sense of celebrating the intensity of the passing relationship that haunts so much of her work. No wonder Ross is (was?) so important in gay male scene culture, for she both reflects what that culture takes to be an inevitable reality (that relationships don't last) and at the same time celebrates it, validates it.

Not all disco music works in this vein, yet in both some of the more sweetly melancholy orchestrations (even of lively numbers, like 'You Should Be Dancing' in *Saturday Night Fever*) and some of the lyrics and general tone (e.g. Donna Summer's *Four Seasons of Love* album), there is a carry-over of this emotional timbre. At a minimum then, disco's romanticism provides an embodiment and validation of an aspect of gay culture.

But romanticism is a particularly paradoxical quality of art to come to terms with. Its passion and intensity embody or create an experience that negates the dreariness of the mundane and everyday. It gives us a glimpse of what it means to live at the height of our emotional and experiential capacities – not dragged down by the banality of organized routine life. Given that everyday banality, work, domesticity, ordinary sexism and racism, are rooted in the structures of class and gender of this society, the flight from that banality can be seen as – is – a flight from capitalism and patriarchy themselves as lived experiences.

What makes this more complicated is the actual situation within which disco occurs. Disco is part of the wider to-and-fro between work and leisure, alienation and escape, boredom and enjoyment that we are so accustomed to (and which *Saturday Night Fever* plugs into so effectively). Now this to-and-fro is partly the mechanism by which we keep going, at work, at home – the respite of leisure gives us the energy for work, and anyway we are still largely brought up to think of leisure as a 'reward' for work. The circle locks us into it. But what happens in that space of leisure can be profoundly significant – it is there that we may learn about an alternative to work and to society as it is. Romanticism is one of the major modes of leisure in which this sense of an alternative is kept alive. Romanticism asserts that the limits of work and domesticity are not the limits of experience.

I don't say that the passion and intensity of romanticism is a political ideal we could strive for – I doubt that it is humanly possible to live permanently at this pitch. What I do believe is that the movement between banality and something 'other' than banality is an essential dialectic of society, a constant keeping open of a gap between what is and what could or should be. Herbert Marcuse in the currently unfashionable *One-Dimensional Man* argues that our society tries to close that gap, to assert that what is is all that there could be, is what should be. For all its commercialism and containment within the work:leisure to-and-fro, I think disco romanticism is one of the things that can keep the gap open, that can allow the *experience of contradiction* to continue. Since I also believe that political struggle is rooted in experience (though utterly doomed if left at it), I find this dimension of disco potentially positive. (A further romantic/utopian aspect of disco is realized in the non-commercial discos organized by gay and women's groups. Here a moment of community can be achieved, often in circle dances or simply in the sense of knowing people as people, not anonymous bodies. Fashion is less important, and sociability correspondingly more so. This can be achieved in smaller clubs, perhaps especially outside the centre of London, which, when not just grotty monuments to self-oppression, can function as supportive expressions of something like a gay community.)

Materialism

Disco is characteristic of advanced capitalist societies simply in terms of the scale of money squandered on it. It is a riot of consumerism, dazzling in its technology (echo chambers, double and more tracking, electric instruments), overwhelming in its scale (banks of violins, massed choirs, the limitless range of percussion instruments), lavishly gaudy in the mirrors and tat of discothèques, the glitter and denim flash of its costumes. Its tacky sumptuousness is well evoked in the film *Thank God It's Friday*. Gone are the restraint of popular song, the sparseness of rock and reggae, the simplicity of folk. How can a socialist, or someone trying to be a feminist, defend it?

In certain respects, it is doubtless not defensible. Yet socialism and feminism are both forms of materialism – why is disco, a celebration of materiality if ever there was one, not therefore the appropriate art form of materialist politics?

Partly, obviously, because materialism in politics is not to be confused with mere matter. Materialism seeks to understand how things are in terms of how they have been produced and constructed in history, and how they can be better produced and constructed. This certainly does not mean immersing oneself in the material world – indeed, it includes deliberately stepping back from the material world to see what makes it the way it is and how to change it. Yes, but, materialism is also based on the profound conviction that politics is about the material world, and indeed that human life and the material world are all there is, no God, no magic forces. One of the dangers of materialist politics is that it is in constant danger of spiritualizing itself, partly because of the historical legacy of the religious forms that brought materialism into existence, partly because materialists have to work so hard not to take matter at face value that they often end up not treating it as matter at all. Disco's celebration of materiality is only a celebration of the world we are necessarily and always immersed in, and disco's materiality, in its technological modernity, is resolutely historical and cultural – it can never be, as most art claims for itself, an 'emanation' outside of history and of human production.

Disco's combination of romanticism and materialism effectively tells us – lets us experience – that we live in a world of materiality, that we can enjoy materiality but that the experience of materiality is not necessarily what the everyday world assures us it is. Its eroticism allows us to rediscover our bodies as part of this experience of materiality and the possibility of change.

If this sounds over the top, let one thing be clear – disco can't change the world, make the revolution. No art can do that, and it is pointless expecting it to. But partly by opening up experience, partly by changing definitions, art, disco, can be used. To which one might risk adding the refrain – If it feels good, *use* it.

Gay Left 8, 1979

References

Marcuse, Herbert (1968) *One-Dimensional Man*, London: Sphere

Further reading

Frith, Simon (1981) *Sound Effects*, London: Constable.
Gill, John (1995) 'Nightclubbing' in *Queer Noises: Male and Female Homosexuality in Twentieth Century Music*, London: Cassell, 134–42.
Savage, Jon (1990) 'Tainted love: the influence of male homosexuality and sexual divergence on pop music and culture since the war', in Alan Tomlinson (ed.) *Consumption, Identity and Style*, London: Routledge.

Thomas, Anthony (1995) 'The house the kids built: the gay Black imprint on American dance music' in Creekmur, Corey K. and Doty, Alexander (eds), *Out in Culture: Gay Lesbian and Queer Essays on Popular Culture*, Durham, NC: Duke University Press, 437–45.

17

GETTING OVER THE RAINBOW

Identity and pleasure in gay cultural politics

The 1970s saw the growth of many forms of cultural politics. Not since the years immediately following the Russian Revolution have socialists been so heavily and actively aware of the importance of cultural politics. The gay movement has had a special role to play here, above all in showing how a politics of culture can be rooted in, and grow out of, the already existing culture of an oppressed group. The gay movement activated the political potential of what lesbians and gay men had already achieved in developing against the grain of oppression: a particular way of life, a culture. I want to argue that this relation between a movement and the lived culture of the group that it represents can serve as an object lesson for the left. In addition, I suggest that the particular concerns of identity and pleasure, brought to political flower from the ground of the gay subculture, indicate specific ways of connecting political aims with the way people actually think and feel about their lives.

The development of gay culture is a classic instance of Marx's dictum that 'people make their own history, but they do not make it just as they please; they do not make it under circumstances chosen by themselves, but under circumstances directly encountered, given and transmitted from the past' (Marx 1977: 96). This is a dictum that all branches of the left need to integrate into their thinking and their political agenda.

The case of lesbians and gay men is exemplary but also extreme, in the sense that culture *is* the situation of gay people. Gays are defined and structurally placed in the sphere of culture – there are the circumstances that are not of our own choosing. Having been so placed, gays have sought to gain control over those conditions and in the process have produced a wealth of new cultural forms, new definitions of identity, new awarenesses of human happiness.

To understand this further, we need to consider first the question of the very concept 'homosexual', before going on to the issue of why culture is so privileged an arena of gay movement activity and the significance of some of the forms it takes. It is wrong to think of homosexuality – or almost any

161

aspect of human body activity – as a biological given. Rather, we need to consider how 'the homosexual' has emerged historically as a *social construct* an idea, and also a way of placing people socially, which has only come about in the last two centuries. There are two main points to stress when making this argument.

First, it is clear that bodily (including genital) contact between persons of the same sex is indeed universal. However, just as with bodily contact between persons of the opposite sex, same sex contact never exists outside a particular social formation. No body contact ever occurs in a social vacuum, and hence is never experienced in a purely 'biological' way. Thus although same sex body contact occurs throughout all history (and incidentally in the animal kingdom) it is never in any given instance ahistorical. What is remarkable about developments since the eighteenth century is the way that body activity has been narrowed down to be also the designation of a certain sort of person. Where once same sex body contact might be recognized as an activity (albeit, in our society, sinful) that people might be involved in, now there is a term, 'the homosexual', for persons who are socially/clinically defined as those who habitually involve themselves in same sex contact. 'Homosexual', a nineteenth-century coinage, designates persons not acts.

Part of the reason for using the laborious mouthful 'same sex body contact' is now I hope evident. It is a problem to use the word 'homosexual' outside the historical period of the word's currency, for we risk blurring the very point that needs to be made, namely that 'homosexuality', as our society calls it and understands it, did not exist outside the actual existence of the word. There is a further reason for avoiding the term – and indeed, now, politically, shunning it – and that is that it focuses so exclusively on the element of genital contact. This leads us to the second stage of the argument about the concept of the homosexual.

The word 'sexual' is notoriously hard to handle, since what one person finds sexual another does not. However, in general usage, the word does imply some degree of genital arousal and activity. There is no reason why we should not have a word that focuses on one particular body organ, but the word, and the history that surrounds it, has the effect of privileging genital functions over all others. Thus bodily relations between persons of the same sex, once they are designated 'homosexual', come to be seen entirely in terms of genitality. This is so even when actual genital activity is felt not to have taken place, as in the common supposed defence of homosexuals (and especially lesbians) that 'it's all right, they don't *do* anything'. This is a doubly offensive, and symptomatic, lie, since it both assumes genital activity would be wrong and at the same time implies that 'doing' and 'screwing' are synonymous, as if the limit of body relations between the same sex is genital. The power of ideas of sexuality is quite extraordinary, for not only do they focus attention on the genitals to the exclusion of all else, but they also have a tendency to reduce other aspects of human life to genital activity. This permeates common-sense thought. How often in conversation are a person's motives construed in terms of sexual desire, how often people's problems assumed to be sexual at root. It has become a habit in western society to look to sexuality as the explain-all of life, to see the fulfilment and frustration of genital desire as the key to the truth about what people want in general, what they do and what they are.

That 'the homosexual' is a modern social category, and that sexuality is a word with attendant institutional and social support that privileges the genitals in our understanding of the human body and its relation to being human: these two ideas inform most of what follows. One point must be made clear. The fact that 'the homosexual' and 'sexuality' have just been discussed as ideas does not mean that they exist in a realm of pure spirit. They are ideas by which we live. They are the very means by which we know our place in society and experience our bodies. I live my life in those terms, though in constant struggle within and against them. I do think of myself as a homosexual or, on better days, as gay, and I feel defined as a person by those sexual designations and observe that that is how I am treated too. And I habitually over-privilege genital response and often conflate it with sensual, sensuous and emotional response. What I have just written is a personal way of stating the kinds of issue that I now wish to sketch out about gay cultural politics.

The centrality of culture

Before looking at possible reasons why culture is so central to the gay movement, it would be as well to say something briefly about what I mean the terms 'culture' and 'gay culture' to refer to. I am using 'culture' in the very widest sense to refer not only to the arts but to all those products and practices that both express and constitute the forms, values and emotional structures of social life. The specific references I shall be making to gay culture will hardly touch 'the arts' at all, but will discuss for reasons that will be spelt out later, dress, dancing, forms of relating in public and ways of using and relating to the human body. These are particular instances of the various and manifold forms and activities that constitute gay ways of making sense of the world.

It is important to stress that gay culture does not necessarily know itself as political, much less as politically progressive or socialist. But we cannot afford, anywhere on the left, to be dismissive of the way life is felt, thought and lived by both the people we represent and ourselves. It is within culture that homosexual identities and pleasures are formed. When I use the term 'gay culture', I mean to indicate *any* cultural practice that may be considered significantly homosexual, whether or not it is a radical practice. The term 'gay cultural politics' I restrict to cultural work within the gay movement itself or markedly informed by its perspectives. Again, such activity may well not be radical. It could also be purely reformist or else more centred on individualistic 'revolt' or on the creation of alternative life-styles *within* society as it is.

Reasons why culture is central to the gay movement can be approached through slightly different notions of what the word 'culture' means. First culture can be used to refer to the ways in which a society thinks and feels about itself. It is the ensemble of ideas, representations and forms that are available to people in a society to make sense of themselves and their society. Culture is not innocent. It is grounded in the interests of the people who produce it and in this sense it is a very similar concept to that of ideology. Like ideology, culture does not operate in a unitary way within a society: it involves contradictions and often antagonisms both within and between social groupings – along lines of class, gender, race and such socially designated factors as sexual orientation. The advantage of the word 'culture' in the present context, rather than ideology, is that it insists on the *material* and *affective* dimension of making sense as well as on the *cognitive*.

Culture in this sense is where and how the very concept and definition of homosexuality are produced. Precisely because, as I have argued, homosexuality is not a biological given, any politics based upon or around it is already a politics of culture, a politics centred on the sense made of particular potentials of the body. Gay politics is always already cultural politics, whether we like it or not.

Second, the word 'culture' can also designate that sphere of life that is left over when the realm of necessity has been fulfilled. It is the realm of feelings, pleasure, reflection, leisure. It is of course entirely wrong to think that such things do not permeate every aspect of human existence, but a predominant and effective way of thinking about our lives puts necessity in one slot and culture in another. Necessity includes work to *produce* the maintenance of life, and the family and kinship to *reproduce* life. And by very definition gays are seen as being outside these.

But such struggles as the Gay Rights at Work Committee and the campaigns around lesbian mothers brilliantly disrupt the distinction between necessity and culture, between gays and productive/reproductive life. They demonstrate that gays are involved in the labour process and that gays do bear and bring up children. By insisting on gay rights at work, we insist that sexuality and emotion do not evaporate when we clock in but inform every aspect of life. By fighting for the rights of lesbians (and gay men) to the custody and care of children, we refuse the idea that heterosexual intercourse and a concern for life are the same thing.

Much of the 'public' panic surrounding such struggles derives from the way they blur the distinction between sexuality as a private, personal domain and work and procreation as public and socially responsible. This panic serves to reinforce the idea that gays, by virtue of their sexuality, are to be defined as irrelevant to work and impossible as parents. *As gays* they are to be defined outside production and reproduction. The institutions of the law, social welfare, family organization, and so on, serve to keep us outside productive/reproductive life. Our identity as *gay* is experienced by ourselves and others as in a very different relationship to our identity as worker or parent (or relative). The space we occupy and the space in which we must struggle is therefore primarily the space outside of 'necessity', the space of culture.

Identity

If 'the homosexual' is a social category, then it is evident that actual people who fall into that category are going to be identified with and by it. People grow up to learn that they are homosexual or queer, or gay, and it is with this homosexual identity that gay political culture must necessarily engage.

Gay politics is about transcending the historical category 'homosexual', but it has always been a mistake to imagine that there could be an immediate, magic transcendence, a sudden leap free from the cultural categories within which we think, feel, live and are. Gay politics has necessarily to start from the given category, even if it ultimately wishes to move beyond it. This is not just a question of the political distinction between tactics (accepting and defending the category) and strategy (transcending it). It is only by accepting the category that we can transcend it. This is not idly said. To deny the category is to avoid the actual reality of the situation, namely, that certain people are *placed* in the category 'homosexual', and to ignore a situation is the surest way of ensuring that it remains the same.

What is at stake, to begin with, is who controls the definition of the category. The key significance of the gay movement is that for the first time in living memory, gay people *themselves* determined that they would decide the definition. The major, though by no means wholly secure, victory of this process has been the social acceptance of the word 'gay'. To have reached a point where a word selected by an oppressed group to describe itself is used almost as normal not only on the left but very generally in the media and in conversation is an extraordinary achievement. It signals the first occasion that people designated as homosexual have turned round and determined that they would decide what it means to be so designated.

Struggles over words can often seem trivial. Endlessly correcting people's assumptions that I must be married or have a girlfriend is tiring for me and seems niggling to those I'm correcting. Yet such relentlessness is needed to change ingrained habits of thought, for habits are so hard to change. Word struggles often have a wider resonance. I remember going on a demonstration against the Industrial Relations Bill where people had placards saying 'We're here for the queer', an attack on the prime minister, Edward Heath. By asking (successfully) for them to be removed we made a connection between sexism and labour politics, all by objecting to a word. (Similarly, we should object to attacks on Thatcher for being female or on Reagan for being old – there's enough to attack without falling into sexism and ageism.)

Being socially categorized, and determining something of the form of that categorization, also provides the possibility of thinking in terms of collective action. It is by recognizing that one's problems are not unique, that one belongs to a social group, that one is able to think in terms of together changing a general situation rather than accepting a purely personal 'condition'. Gay cultural politics has been particularly important here in exploring new identities, new shared senses of who we are.

An example of what I mean are the debates in the gay movement that surround disco. Disco has been a major development in gay culture in the 1970s and the wider disco scene itself grew out of, and is still marked by, gay disco. It is probably the most widespread form of leisure activity that gays are involved in, as both a dance/music form of expression and a space for social and sexual contact. The precise form it takes is important for the gay movement, because that is where so many gays 'are at'. I mean this both literally and figuratively: gays are in discos in vast numbers, and disco culture means a lot to us. Disco is, quantitatively and qualitatively, where we can reach gay people. The discussions at gay movement meetings about disco are often apparently focused on problems of organization – for instance, whether to charge, whether to hold discos in a straight or a gay venue, who will supply the music, etc. But at bottom they are about the business of constructing a gay identity. Thus some people argue that we should take our cue from the existing gay scene saying that there are certain ways of coping, forms of friendship network, the gay bar or club serving as a kind of community, that we could learn from. And they also point out that the kind of music favoured, usually derived from black music, is in some sense a gay music, and hence already expressive of a gay identity. Others point to the exploitativeness and furtiveness of the gay scene, the predominance of men and masculine modes of behaviour, and want the gay movement to learn from the counter-culture and its life-styles. The result is alternative discos, at their best a creative fusion or interplay of both of these traditions. The experience of being with gay people is altered, for instance, if the discos are free, if people talk to each other, if they are obviously organized by other gay people, if women and men are equally welcome and made welcome, if people dance in circles instead of either isolated or in couples. Talking about and dancing to different sorts of music can explore or reinforce sexual identities. The wrangling about whether to let Donna Summer or the Rolling Stones predominate is a way of talking through what we want our identity to be. Summer represents disco, an already gay cultural form, at its most sensuous; the Stones represent rock'n'roll at its most 'alternative' but also its most 'straight' (in sexual terms). They are emblematic of different ways of being. Discussing and dancing to them become the very activity of constructing a shared sense of who we are.

Another example which brings out the interplay between pre-political sub-cultural forms and the construction of new identities is the question of dress. Dress is always a significant aspect of a person, for it reveals class, gender, racial and other subcultural positions whether consciously or unconsciously. Importantly it indicates how the wearer inhabits those positions, how she/he feels about being in that social position. Dress is especially significant for gays since being gay doesn't actually of itself 'show' physically, and it is only through dress that we can make a statement about ourselves that, unlike a verbal pronouncement, is there all the time.

The gay movement could draw on styles of dress that were already developed in the gay subculture, for instance, various forms of drag and prettiness for men, of butch and dyke gear for women. These styles provided a ground for a gay cultural politics of dress. Even before it is self-consciously political, drag and dyke dress is a play with the signs of femininity and masculinity, with what is appropriate dress for 'real' women and men. Gay cultural politics, in its concern with dress, has kept putting these definitions of gender in question. I do not mean to imply that confrontationist drag and dyke gear necessarily makes onlookers think through their own gender identities. Cultural struggle does not work automatically like that, much as many fondly hope it does. But such tactics are part of a wider debate about how and what it is to be a man or a woman, and how the very definitions of femininity and masculinity are posited on heterosexuality. This is to make it sound like an intellectual issue. But the point is rather, that gay cultural politics actually involves considering how you dress, being sensitive to what you and others wear. And this means bearing a consciousness of the categories of gender and sexuality in the lived texture of appearances.

One could make a similar argument around the current 'masculinization' of the gay male style. Today, gay men are rather more likely to adopt a macho look than drag and prettiness. This too is in a sense a reversal of the signs of masculinity. Gender roles are crucially defined in terms of heterosexuality – 'men', as a social category, are people who screw 'women'. By taking the signs of masculinity and eroticizing them in a blatantly homosexual context, much mischief is done to the security with which 'men' are defined in society, and by which their power is secured. If that bearded, muscular beer-drinker turns out to be a pansy, however are you going to know the 'real' men any more? From this too stem the play, exaggeration and parody of much contemporary gay masculinization. The most widely known example of this is the disco group Village People, whose dress draws on all the stereotypes of ultra-masculinity in a camped-up flauntingly gay way (Figure 17.1). There is profound ambivalence in this development. I am not at all clear in my own mind how gay men do actually relate to this masculinization. It can be taken straight – as a worship of the signs of male power, as an attempt to prove 'I may be queer but I'm still a man'. But it can be taken ironically and reflexively too, and two things help to encourage

Figure 17.1 The Village People

this. One is the debate about dress that the gay movement set in motion.
People go on talking about the significance of what they wear, and how it
does or does not carry and reproduce male power in society. Second, there is
camp, that characteristically gay repertoire of parody, wit, put-down and
send-up. This remains a powerful strain in gay culture, and it has always
shown both a great sensitivity to gender roles *as* roles and a refusal to take
the trappings of femininity and masculinity too seriously. We have to try to
understand the new macho look in relation to all the frames of reference,
reactionary and subversive, that can inform it.

Pleasure

Disco and dress are examples of the way that gay cultural politics is centrally
concerned with the contestation of identities. These identifies make collective action possible, as the much more confident burgeoning of gay culture
with a strong activist current in the USA makes clear. Gay cultural politics
is also about pleasure. There is a definite fit between the gay movement's
basic concern with sexuality and the centrality of culture to its political practice. Both are to do with pleasure. However, pleasure remains a forbidden
term of reference, particularly on the left. Pleasure is something you can

168

guiltily have, or have after the important things, or get as a reward for doing other things. As itself a goal, it is still not, to speak paradoxically, taken seriously. And nowhere is this more true than on the left.

It was clear from the start that the gay movement was primarily and perhaps exclusively concerned with sexuality and the consequences of a particular choice of sexuality. The women's movement has also been centrally concerned with sexuality, but women *as* women are not oppressed uniquely or even primarily in terms of their sexual desires but in terms of not being men. Struggles around housework, equal pay, job opportunities and so on do not spring directly from sexual activity. Even those struggles that are essentially concerned with sexuality somehow manage to couch themselves in other terms. Thus, issues of contraception, abortion and nursery facilities tend to run together and to be argued for in terms of what constitutes sane and healthy childcare and how such things free women in relation to paid employment, creativity and so on, rather than in terms of such things making sexuality less attendant with procreative anxiety, more controllable, more *enjoyable*. I know that that argument is there, but none the less that is not, overall, how the debates around the issues developed. None of this could be said of gay movement issues. Queer-bashing, police harassment, discrimination in employment, treatment in the media, and all the other areas of gay activism may have the same civil rights flavour, but they all stem from the assertion of the right to a certain form of sexual activity. Nor was the gay movement merely demanding the right and need to love members of the same sex, but to enjoy sex with them. When in 1972 the Birmingham Gay Liberation Front produced the first British gay sex education pamphlet, *Growing Up Homosexual*, pleasure was listed as the first and overriding function of sex, above the expression of love and (a poor third) procreation. Many in the movement pushed further, to insist that promiscuity, one-night stands, masturbation, forms of sexuality with minimal, attenuated, or non-existent human relationship elements, were as valid as, or more valid than, monogamy, affairs and love. They were seen as being in some sense more 'direct' and 'honest', less involved in manipulation and hypocrisy.

As Simon Watney points out, the Gay Liberation Front (GLF), which was the most vocal and 'radical' of the gay movement's various forms, saw sexuality as very much more than a particular activity. Sexuality was seen as the key that would unlock the fragmentation and alienation of advanced capitalist patriarchy.

> Gay Liberation attempted to recuperate an illusion. That illusion maintained that our sexuality is the single most determining aspect of our entire existence.
>
> (1980: 72)

He argues persuasively that a great deal more was felt to be at stake in strug-
gling around sexuality than the pleasure of sexual activity for itself. This is
clear too from Aubrey Walter's introduction to *Come Together*, a selection of
articles from the GLF newspaper (1980) – though he is less critical of GLF's
position than is Simon Watney. But GLF was not the whole gay movement,
and a far more widespread impulse behind the various gay political activities of the 1970s was the assertion of the pleasure of sexuality and the right
to that pleasure.

The problem was, again, definition: how to define sexuality. In practice, it
meant genital, orgasmic sexuality. In the relation between women and men
in the gay movement, this led to some pretty conundrums. On the one hand,
in the sexual ideology we inherited, genital sexuality was 'masculine': women
were supposed to be: romantic, their genital sexuality ineluctably intertwined
with love; mysterious, their sexuality not physiologically locatable; or vagi-
nal, a non-starter orgasmically (though not necessarily experienced as such
(cf. McIntosh 1976)). Male gay culture teetered for a long time on the brink
of this inheritance. Some of us wanted to insist on wider notions of sexuality, perhaps feeling there was something to learn from these definitions of
female sexuality. Thus there were references to the 'tyranny of the orgasm'
and a rejection of the instrumental, goal-oriented approach to coupling.
Others wanted to expand the area of genital sexuality, to insist on the validity of more and 'purely' sexual genital activity. Many women were bored by
this internal male debate and also put off by the obsession with genitals.

On the other hand . . . I remember talking to a woman friend of mine
about the tyranny of the orgasm and being told, 'Don't knock orgasms – it
took some of us a long time to get them.' To move beyond genital sexuality
is an achievement for some men; to achieve genital sexuality can be a move
beyond for some women.

We have certainly not succeeded in unpicking these contradictions, and
this is partly because the whole debate, the very use of the word 'sexual', is
still not extricated from the very ideology, discussed above, that separates
genital sexuality from the rest of the body. Once this separation happens we
are left in a quandary, having to choose between either genitality ('masculine') or emotionality ('feminine'), with no room for anything in between.
Like the wider culture of heterosexual permissiveness, much of male gay
culture, with its panoply of commercially supported saunas, bars, clubs and
cruising places, is always in danger of simply wanting to expand genitality,
simply to want more and more of it or to give it the creative power to transcend the present order. A danger, however, is not the whole story. Much
that is happening is also seeking to break down the category 'sexuality',
understood as '*genital* sexuality', and replace it with a new understanding
and experience of the body in human existence.

Body politics

Many aspects of gay culture are a body culture, discovering and constructing new possibilities for the body. Disco and dress, already discussed, are in part about, respectively, the pleasure to be gained from using all one's body and the meanings to be constructed in the imaginative use of dress as body decoration. Massage and body awareness groups actively and consciously produce knowledge of what the body is and can be. More open kissing and hugging between men and men, women and women, are part of the style of the gay movement, both as a public sign that we are gay, but also as a pleasurable experience of friendship and solidarity. Such things begin to create a culture that refuses to refuse the body any more.

Many may well want to label all this bourgeois individualism. Doesn't it smack of California, where the sun always shines and people vote for Reagan? Isn't it the most gross self-indulgence in an age of mass unemployment and economic recession? Certainly it is hard to keep one's eyes on the wider goals of sexual politics when these immediate, hard issues face one. And yet to refuse this explanation of the body is simply to buy back into the cycle of body control that *constitutes* contemporary society.

Society isn't one thing and the human body another. Society is the organization of the human body, how we experience our bodies and what we do to and with them. The human body is a basic unit in any social formation. The paid worker's body, the houseworker's body remain the essential elements of any economy, of any maintenance and reproduction of life. In this society, the use of our bodies is compartmentalized: certain limbs and organs are used for work and nothing else, while pleasure is focused on an ever-narrowing range of 'erogenous' areas. Except when they occur in important activities such as sport and dance, all other body potentials are unknown, unrecognized, marginalized. Such compartmentalization produces body units that are easy to control; it rationalizes the fluidity and range of body potential. It also makes of the body something easier to place in economic exchange relations. It is easier to buy a person's body skill than her/his whole body. It is easier to sell pleasure if you are trying to appeal to one clearly defined region of the body.

This last point has led to the greatest confusion in the development of male gay sexual practices in the past ten years. Because the early gay movement put so much emphasis on genital sexuality, it was easy for capitalism to meet its demands. Bars, saunas, pornography, all the institutions of permissiveness, could seem like an answer to the demand for the liberation of sexuality. As long as sexuality meant genital sexuality, it could be quantified and its 'needs' met – more opportunities to do it more often. (There is a similar ideology in women's magazines like *Cosmopolitan*, though not in lesbian publications.) Our mistake, which we are only just beginning to see, was in demanding the liberation of sexuality, when we need to be demanding liberation *from* sexuality, in the name of the body.

The women's movement has long recognized the political importance of the body. Struggles around contraception, abortion, wife-battering and rape are not just 'issues' to form the basis of verbal, moral discussion nor are they only – though this they crucially are – assertions of the individual's right to determine what happens to her body. They also make us see how the very organization of procreation, the family and sexuality in society is done with, through and often to women's *bodies*. Though men find this especially hard to come to terms with and live with, such organization is also done with, through and to their own bodies. Men's physical frustrations and anxieties may have ideological or psychic roots, but where they get expressed is the body.

Ignorance of this on the left constitutes a denial of the body that is fatal for the movement. It means that we neither know our bodies for what they are and can be, nor do we operate effectively in and with them. In an immediate sense, denial of the body may simply make us less efficient in day-to-day political work: more liable to be tired, to be late, to be irritable, to be uncomradely. In the long term, denial of the body means that we do not take possession of our bodies politically.

'Body politics' is not an idle phrase. It points to the way in which society attempts to make over every person into a cog in an efficient system that at the same time fragments any control or knowledge we may have over or of our bodies. Our bodies are the site of control and power. We are not disembodied economic counters or ideological constructs. Lack of body politics has allowed left theory to lurch through various kinds of idealism, though each one calls itself materialist.

On the one hand, Marxism can degenerate into economic determinism. This may *appear* very materialist, because it is dealing with the 'hard' realities of money and work, but it deals with these realities in an abstracted idealist way. Economic determinism reduces everything to the economic rather than seeing things *in relation to* the economic (and much else besides). It does designate economic categories and chart economic structures, but frequently fails to connect with the realities of factory and office life, the problems of getting and spending money. In other words, it fails to understand how economic structures are *lived and affected* in the skin and bones of people working.

On the other hand, recent Marxist theorists have rightly rejected such economic reductionism. But in their search for an alternative theory, they have come up with one that is equally prone to idealism. Working from theories of language and from psychoanalysis of a certain kind, they have put a valuable stress on the role of ideology in history, and, in particular, on the way people are socially formed into what we understand people to be – what is called 'the construction of the subject'. Yet their theory leads to a position where being 'a person' or 'a subject' is *only* a construction in language and ideology. Granted that society fashions us through words and representation of humanness, but it fashions us out of flesh and blood, not thin air.

None of this means that what the human body is is simply what 'nature' makes it. To go back to the point made at the beginning of this article, the biological activity of pleasurable bodily contact between persons of the same sex does not automatically give us the concepts 'sexuality' and 'the homosexual'. Those concepts are attempts to make sense (however, in this case, cock-eyed . . .) out of what are real biological activities. What is at stake is that, first, we are animals and can learn something about our bodies from biology. Second, that whatever else may come into play in the organization of our animal bodies to become specifically human bodies, we none the less remain in those bodies and had better learn about them: learn about what is biologically given, what is ideologically fashioned in them, if we want to be effective in history. And being effective in history is a cornerstone of what I take socialism to be about.

Gay culture, even when fully informed by sexual and socialist politics, does not have all the answers. But it does ask some of the questions, it does begin to think through not only gay identities, but *all* sexual and gender identities, and not only to think them through but to live them through the culture of the body. By so doing we make the very stuff of the social formation, our bodies, less amenable to prevailing power structures, more resistant to oppressive definitions and maimed existences. And in the pleasure we get we also get a glimpse of the other end of the rainbow.

From George Bridges and Rosalind Brunt (eds) *Silver Linings*,
London: Lawrence & Wishart, 1981

References

McIntosh, Mary (1976) 'Sexuality', *Papers on Patriarchy*, Lewes, Sussex: Women's Publishing Collective, 73–5.

Marx, Karl (1977) 'The eighteenth brumaire of Louis Bonaparte', in Karl Marx and Friedrich Engels, *Selected Works*, London: Lawrence & Wishart, 93–179.

Walter Aubrey (1980) *Come Together*, London: Gay Men's Press.

Watney Simon (1980) 'The ideology of GLF', in Gay Left Collective (eds) *Homosexuality: Power and Politics*, London: Allison & Busby, 64–76.

Further reading

Bersani, Leo (1989) 'Is the rectum a grave?', in Douglas Crimp (ed.) *AIDS: Cultural Analysis, Cultural Activism*, Cambridge, MA: MIT Press, 197–222.

Bristow, Joseph (1989) 'Being gay: politics, identity, pleasure', *New Formations* 9: 61–81.

Bronski, Michael (1984) *Culture Clash: the Making of a Gay Sensibility*, Boston, MA: South End Press.

Cohen, Derek and Dyer, Richard (1980) 'The politics of gay culture', in Gay Left Collective (eds) *Homosexuality: Power and Politics*, London: Allison & Busby, 172–86.

Jay, Karla and Young, Allen (eds) (1978) *Lavender Culture*, New York: Harcourt, Brace, Jovanovich.

Shepherd, Simon and Wallis, Mick (eds) (1989) *Coming On Strong: Gay Politics and Culture,* London: Unwin Hyman.
Weeks, Jeffrey (1985) *Sexuality and its Discontents*, London: Routledge & Kegan Paul.
Weeks, Jeffrey (1986) *Sexuality*, London: Tavistock.

18

THE WANING OF
ENTERTAINMENT

Entertainment of the kind discussed in these pages depends for its forms and appeals on the notion of escapism, and this in turn entails a sense of there being something that is not entertainment, that needs to be escaped from. Entertainment is thus apart, different, special, a treat. Yet the bases for that sense of entertainment have undergone such profound alterations in the past half-century that entertainment may now be ceasing to be a viable cultural category.

There is no decline, for those with money and access, in the taking of pleasure. On the contrary, we may have entered the most hedonistic period the world has ever known. The word entertainment can be, and always has been, used to speak of the many ways in which people may take pleasure – we entertain people with dinner, in jokes and gossip, we entertain ourselves in hobbies and sports. In this widest sense there is no decline in entertainment; indeed, quite the reverse. What may be in eclipse, though, is the provision of entertainment in artefacts and performances based on a dynamic of separation and escape. This can be traced in technological, geographic and social developments as well as in changes in the content and forms of the arts and media.

Before the 1920s, entertainment was something you went to or perhaps did at home on special occasions. Theatre, music hall, concerts, film were, typically, all performances housed elsewhere, not where you lived or worked, and done at particular times. I don't want to oversimplify the account – people performed for each other at home on occasion, in some cases quite often; there were entertainments that were ongoing and which you could drop into when it suited you (the novel is the quintessential example, but also much theatre and opera was treated like this and music hall, the *café chantant* and burlesque were largely based on the assumption of it). Nonetheless, the dominant practice and definition of entertainment were provided by professionals in spaces and at times neither domestic nor work related (the two latter spaces and times being identical for a majority of women and servants).

The gramophone and radio were the first technologies to alter this. Entertainment was still professionally provided but now it was in the home and sometimes in the workplace and could be had at any time. If in practice, initially, radio took its cue for the broadcasting timetable from the wider pattern of work and leisure, it always had, and soon realized, the potential for being continuously available, at which point you could leave it on all the time if you wanted. This elision of the space–time of entertainment with that of home, work and other forms of leisure was most obvious in the if desired, ubiquity and continuousness of music, which then became yet more pervasive in the development of muzak (all built environments could have music all the time) and the personal stereo (you could have music where you were at any time).

Speech and music lend themselves especially well to this development because you don't have, as with vision, to focus an organ on them – you hear things without having to turn your ears to them, whereas you can only see things if you look at them. Only posters, usually advertising, provide the kind of visual wallpaper in public spaces equivalent to the aural wallpaper of muzak and the Walkman. Nevertheless, television, video and the internet are visual as well as audio media that are also in the home, permanently available, that you can take about with you and access at any time. In all these contexts, although both sound and audio-visual performance are still professionally provided and may be a means of escape from (distraction from, cutting one off from) the cares of life, it is no longer spatially and temporally separate from the rest of life. Besides, with the internet, performance is not even necessarily professionally provided (except by technicians facilitating commercial web sites) – music, drama, all kinds of performances and visual expressions are now as likely to be amateur as professional, and anyone may be both a provider and a consumer of entertainment.

These changes in the time and place of pleasurable performances are of a piece with changes in the social organization of production and consumption. Because of a combination of the restructuring of work (part-time, temporary, multiple, franchising, consultancy and so on) and technological developments (voicemail, telephone phone conferencing, mobile phones, fax, email, websites), more people work at home, while changes in the philosophy of management have emphasized flexible hours, networking, relaxation spaces and dehierarchization in the workplace. Work is either interleaved with leisure, all in the same space, or is barely distinguishable from it. Workstation work especially, and despite the name, may be an endless flipping between email (business and gossip), cruising the net (for business and fun), games, spreadsheets, calculations and word-processing. Childcare is similarly diffused, neither wholly absorbing women's domestic space and time nor so expansively socialized as in both traditional and alternative (hippie, kibbutz) communities. These developments are profoundly uneven. An army of the underpaid, still predominantly female and/or non-white, picks up the pieces of drudgery, not least in relation to babies and children; the call centres so critical to the new organization of work are themselves policed to prevent any flipping into pleasure; public services, where for long reigned an ideology of doing it out of duty but also interest (aka pleasure), have seen huge expansions in workloads, most of them bureaucratic. Nonetheless, changing patterns of employment and rearing really have for some people eroded the separation of graft and care from pleasure that was a grounding of entertainment's aesthetics of escape.

Along with these socio-techno-geographic changes go widespread cultural changes. Entertainment has got in everywhere. News and documentary are increasingly presented in the same terms as entertainment, using its forms of presentation and also clearing space for news and documentaries actually about entertainment and pleasure. Politics, whether in the stage management of congresses, conferences, campaigns and parliaments or the apparatus of spin and personality, and its inseparability from television, often appears as a branch of show business; even alternative politics is often based on street theatre and the performance of protest. Most interesting, and complex, is sport. This has always occupied a curious place in relation to entertainment: it clearly is entertainment for those who watch it, but it is also related to notions of recreation, health and moral value. Unlike true entertainment, sport is true: for all its performative elements, with their aesthetic and affective dimensions, it is not a representational performance, it is itself; and while the quality and authenticity of all entertainment can be discussed, winning in sport is absolute (even disputing a win is founded on the assumption that there is an absolute win that can be determined). Yet sport, too, has been invaded by entertainment values, in the increasing razzmatazz accompanying many sports, especially in the United States; in its incorporation into entertainment modes in television presentation; in the apparatus of stardom and secondary material; in the recategorization as sports of activities where winning depends on formal judgements (gymnastics, skating, ballroom dancing, formation swimming) or which are widely known to be indeed performances (professional wrestling). Sport does remain special – winning is winning is winning, and even news and documentary continue to address the real unpleasurableness of reality, and politics does still involve the actual exercise of power. Yet the edges of the distinctions are fuzzy. And, to the degree that everything becomes entertainment, entertainment itself ceases to be a category.

The changes in what is provided as entertainment are felt in its representational world. Entertainment classically dealt in glamour, utopia, the exotic, the extraordinary, the exceptional, enjoyment through imagining other worlds or ways of being. However, through the twentieth century, people increasingly wanted to take pleasure in people like themselves, realities like their own. This is a trend already under way in the growth of the novel, even in the eighteenth century. One index of its development is the demystification of stars, no longer seen as special people but just like you and me: Swanson and Dietrich become the Spice Girls via Brigitte Bardot, Valentino becomes Gable becomes Kevin Costner and Tom Hanks. Another index is the centrality of soap to television output, where it is precisely a sense of ordinary, everyday life in its endless ongoingness that is constructed, albeit with varying degrees of fantastification (*Dallas* and *Dynasty*) and something like realism (*Coronation Street*, *Eastenders* and *Brookside*). Though he might turn over in his grave at the thought of it, the declaration by the theorist of Italian neo-realism, Cesare Zavattini, that 'for us everyday life is interesting', has come to partial fruition in the soap, and even more in the fly-on-the-wall documentary or docu-soap. Here actual everyday life is edited into a narrative with real ordinary people playing to camera. The subject matter of entertainment is no longer how much more beautiful or exciting life could be but rather an assurance that life as it is is entertaining.

Yet more remarkable than the triumph of realism as entertainment (where once they had seemed in opposition) is the collapsing of even the distinction between realism and entertainment. The most publicly notable instance of this are shows such as *Big Brother*, *Popstars* and *Survivor*, in which ordinary people (i.e. not professional entertainers) participate in events staged for and wholly acknowledged as television. Though they are referred to as 'reality television', we may need some other term to do the phenomenon justice, since the reality is a reality of television rather than, as previously, a televisual presentation of a reality existing and having its *raison d'être* outside of television. Such programmes do involve winners and those who come out on top are briefly fêted as stars, but what is uppermost is the participants', and the winners', typicality, their ordinariness. It is a kind of mass solipsism, in which we only see apparent reflections of ourselves, warts and all.

Perhaps the most surprising instance of this is the rise of amateur porn. The huge growth of pornography in the 1970s to 1990s involved increasing professionalization, with greater demands on the pulchritude and performance skills of the actors and greater conformity to norms of professional cinema in lighting, stock, *mise en scène* and so on. However, the internet has turned out to be not so much a medium for making such professional porn still more readily available as, rather, the occasion for the explosion of amateur sexual sites. It is as if, given the chance, people don't want to see honed bodies in perfectly oiled couplings but lumpy, scrawny, pimply ordinary bodies doing ordinary things to each other. Pornutopia has become pervasive, habitual exhibitionism and voyeurism.

When pleasure is available anywhere, any time and looks like everywhere and everyone, the dynamic of escape, foundational to entertainment, disappears. Perhaps this more than anything explains the decline of the film musical, which is not only a quintessential entertainment form but also in large part explicitly about entertainment as escape. One of the last musical films to exploit the difference between everyday life and the world of the number was *Saturday Night Fever* (1977) and even here the numbers, the disco routines, were both much more realistically conveyed and emphasized the experience of dancing as much as the display of it. Thereafter films based on music – in this sense musicals – have proliferated but far more in terms of rendering a life pervaded by music than in presenting a movement between the vicissitudes of the narrative and the escape and resolution found in the numbers (e.g. *American Graffiti* (1973), *Car Wash* (1976), *Rumble Fish* (1983), *Something Wild* (1986), *Juice* (1992), *Pulp Fiction* (1994), *Clueless* (1995), *Trainspotting* (1996)).

Like the social, technological and geographic changes to which I have related it, the waning of entertainment is uneven. Musical theatre flourishes (albeit with yearnings towards operatic grandeur), the blockbuster continues to imagine other worlds (*The Matrix, Gladiator*), magic is crucial to the success of shows like *The X-Files, Buffy the Vampire Slayer* and *Charmed* – and anyway most people are not in jobs that seem like play and still need to be taken out of themselves. This is why I speak of entertainment waning, since this both emphasizes the gradualness of the process and, if the metaphor holds true, of the possibility of it being a temporary phase before entertainment waxes again.

Does it matter? For entertainment to wax, do we need drudgery, pain and dreariness to expand, to provide a base from which to escape? Should we not welcome the pleasurization of all aspects of life, even if only, for now, for a minority of the world's population? Is not the rise of pleasure in ordinariness a heartening sign of democracy? Perhaps. Yet the eclipsing of entertainment represents a closing of the gap between an awareness of what is and imagination of what could or should be. Along with education being pressed towards unquestioned instrumental ('vocational') ends, the waning of entertainment risks weakening the ability to be critical of the way things are by feeling how else they might be. And the way things are is that some can live a life that does not need its moments of entertainment while most labour to make it possible. The waning of entertainment might merely confirm the comfortable overclass of Western society in the rightness of its life while extinguishing even the tawdriest visions of happiness for the rest of the world.

INDEX

Page numbers followed by 'ill' refer to illustrations; 'n' refers to a note.

An environmentally friendly book printed and bound in England by www.printondemand-worldwide.com

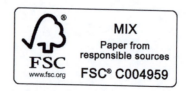
#0328 - - C0 - 234/156/10 - PB